Breakthroughs on Hunger

A JOURNALIST'S ENCOUNTER WITH GLOBAL CHANGE

Richard M. Harley

SMITHSONIAN INSTITUTION PRESS

Washington and London

128761

Illustrations copyright © 1990
John Schreck
Reproduced by permission

Editor: Norman Rudnick
Production Editor: Rebecca Browning
Designer: Alan Carter

Library of Congress Cataloging-in-Publication Data

Harley, Richard M.
Breakthroughs on hunger : a journalist's encounter
with global change / Richard M. Harley.
p.   cm.
Includes index.
ISBN 1-56098-001-X.—ISBN 1-56098-026-5 (pbk.)
1. Rural development—Developing countries—Case studies.
2. Famines—Developing countries—Case studies.   I. Title.
HN981.C6H37   1990
307.1'412'091724—dc20   90-53177

British Library Cataloguing-in-Publication Data available
Manufactured in the United States of America
5 4 3 2 1
94 93 92 91 90

Contents

PART TWO
POWER AND THE POWERLESS

PART THREE
ENERGIES IN THE LEARNING PROCESS

Acknowledgments

The journalist who ventures into uncharted waters will inevitably have patrons of hope who, in some decisive way or moment, encouraged idea to move toward reality. In this I am deeply indebted to distinguished professionals who might easily have had too little time to be encouraging, including Paul Streeten of the World Development Institute, Joyce Moock of the Rockefeller Foundation, Norman Collins of the Ford Foundation, former World Bank president Robert S. McNamara, John Mellor of the International Food Policy Research Institute, Robert Havener at Winrock International, James P. Grant and Tarzie Vittachi of UNICEF, Robert Berg (formerly) of the International Development Conference, my literary agent Marian Young, and colleagues at the Harvard Institute for International Development, including Dwight Perkins, Peter Timmer, Richard Goldman, Tyler Biggs, Pauline Peters, Charles Mann, Malcolm McPherson, Merilee Grindle, and John Cohen.

No less catalytic in this venture have been the financial patrons of hope. They have been as generous in their contribution of ideas as resources—an overflow of their own commitment to a world less fraught with poverty. Here I owe much to the Rockefeller Foundation, the Ford Foundation, the International Fund for Agricultural Development, Carnegie Corporation of New York, UNICEF, and the United Nations Development Programme.

The project has also greatly benefited from the collaboration and financial support of a unique coalition of Christian and Jewish development educators, including those of American Baptist Church, American Friends Service Committee, American Jewish World Service, Bread for the World, Catholic Relief Services, Christian Reform Church, Church of the Brethren, Church World Service, CODEL, Episcopal Church, Evangelical Lutheran Church in America, Mennonite Central Committee, Presbyterian Church in the U.S.A., Seventh-Day Adventist Church, United Church of Christ, United Methodist Church, and U.S. Catholic Conference. Support from MAZON, the Jewish philanthropy, also proved very helpful.

It would be hard to properly credit the enhancements and insights that have come from a host of advisers who gave of their time and energies, including Miguel Altieri, A.T. Ariyaratne, Dennis Avery, Sartaj Aziz, David Bell, Robert Berg, Ela Bhatt, Peter Bourne, Robert Chambers, Lincoln Chen, Marty Chen, Erskine Childers, Kamla Chowdhry, Michael Collinson, William Drayton, Nick Eberstadt, Diogo de Gaspar, John Gerhart, Ricardo Godoy, Neva Goodwin, Lester Gordon, Ramjit Gupta, Malcolm Hall, John Hannah, Mahbub ul Haq, Richard Harwood, Kevin Healy, Peter Hildebrand, Albert Hirschman, David Hopper, Idriss Jazairy, Leobardo Jimenez, Akhter Hameed Khan, David Korten, Raj Krishna, Reggie Laird, Uma Lele, Gilbert Levine, Edwin Martin, Peter Matlon, Larry Minear, Ruth Morgenthau, Thomas Odhiambo, Robert Paarlberg, Marguerite Robinson, Michael Sands, David Seckler, Amartya Sen, John Sewell, D.L. Sheth, Ralph Smuckler, Geeta and A.H. Somjee, Anita Spring, Joseph Stern, Abdelmuhsin al-Sudeary, M.S. Swaminathan, Wayne Swegle, Tom Takami, Judith Tendler, John Thomas, Shadat Ullah, Norman Uphoff, E.T. York, Montague Yudelman, and Edwin Wellhausen.

The editorial and artistic expertise of the Smithsonian Institution Press has made enormous contributions to this volume and its usefulness to readers, as has the able copyediting of Norman Rudnick. Finally, I am deeply grateful for the typing, proofreading, and critical comment of Lynn Mercer and the comment and criticism of Jennifer-Anne B. Foster and Stephen R. Howard. For their invaluable encouragement and support, I thank Isabel F. Bates, David C. Driver, Elizabeth Jacobs, and my parents, who backed this venture all the way.

Introduction

The setting sun had begun its nightly ritual of redecorating Kenya's western highlands, casting long shadows across the rocky green hills and transforming trees into silhouettes against a glowing red sky. Toward the east, a sprawl of clouds hung motionless in a canopy of endless African blue, mirroring the sun's glow. A thousand tiny tree frogs took their cue, and a chorus of soothing high-pitched peeps resonated through the dusk. Jeremiah Rutto suggested we take coffee out to the veranda to watch as night set in. I brought along the shortwave. "Perhaps you'd like to hear a news broadcast from the United States," I said, searching the dial. Dr. Rutto, a research agronomist stationed in the region, flashed the broad smile I had come to associate with Kenyan affirmation. The radio static cleared. A distinctly American accent came through: "We are pleased to bring you a special broadcast—a song just released for simultaneous broadcast on radio stations across the United States, entitled 'We Are the World.' "

Rutto looked puzzled. I tried to explain. "Some popular singers in my country are trying to call people's attention to the needs of famine victims in Ethiopia." The airwaves swelled with celebrity voices and orchestral flourishes that stirred the African night: "We are the world, we are the children, let's start giving." As the celebrities ended their song, Kenya's tree frogs resumed theirs. Jeremiah Rutto seemed still more puzzled. "Well?" I asked, curious for a reaction. "There's just one question," he said. "What do you mean YOU are the world? I thought the goal was helping people to understand Africa and the needs we have *here."* I shifted in my chair to deflect attention from my surprise. A gesture of philanthropy had come across with overtones of cultural superiority. Rutto's smile returned. "Forgive me if I seem uneasy," he said, "but we've seen too much well-intended help for Africa that simply didn't work, or made things worse. There's a huge gap between what people abroad *think* is needed to reduce hunger and poverty, and what it *really* takes, especially out here in the countryside. Even our own leaders, most in the cities, get so far removed from the development struggle that they seldom bridge the gap. Why don't you journalists help people to see what this effort really involves? The difficulties have been formidable. But we *have* learned some things; we're getting somewhere."

Journalists are not known for catering to the wishes of people they meet on assignment. But occasionally the challenge holds out a certain intrigue, and urgency, that cannot be ignored. Rutto's particular words reminded me once again of some very quiet global pursuits that continue to grow more loudly significant in the world poverty equation, but still get far too little public attention. They are pursuits often characterized by two deceptively simple and unarresting little words: "rural development." But in the broader global picture, they refer to a critical search for answers to questions that persist in countries across the developing world: What can be done about the living standards of multitudes of rural people—perhaps as many as two thirds of mankind—who still benefit relatively little from global development? How can a climate of economic opportunity be created to give the rural poor more security, take off the pressure many feel to migrate to already overcrowded cities, and reduce the violence bred in communities that have to endure mass poverty with no end in sight?

Since the 1950s the search for answers has commanded trillions of dollars in aid and technology from the world community and massive efforts from within the poor countries themselves. A surge of new investment came after the world food crisis of 1973 and the growing realization that industrial gains in the cities were not automatically "trickling down" to people in the countryside. Those left out were hundreds of millions of rural families who earn a living off small farms. As late as the mid-'80s, M. S. Swaminathan, one of the leaders of India's Green Revolution, would be warning that much more must be done if talented rural youth are not to leave the coun-tryside in even greater numbers. "We need to give the pursuit of rural development more attractiveness to our rural youth—an image that is intellectually compelling and has the respect it deserves," he said. "Without this, few can be expected to remain in the country-side, or potentials there be released."[1] Leaders of all political ideolo-gies and persuasions have worried about the implications of Third World poverty for global security. As former U.S. Middle East envoy Sol Linowitz once put it, "Despite all the pyrotechnics of the arms race, hunger is the most unsettling force in the world today. Our future depends on how we deal with the contrast between the haves and have-nots."[2]

But Jeremiah Rutto implied that the matter should not always be viewed so ominously. The point was not just that the future would be grim unless something is done; he argued that much is *already* being done, but getting far too little public attention, let alone sup-port. That was 1985. I was, in fact, by then seeking out development strategies on three continents that were reported to have radically improved living standards in the countryside. These so-called excep-tional performers[3] were showing up at different levels of the global development story—from village-based initiatives successful enough to be replicated across wide areas to top-level policy change designed to improve conditions across regions and nations. All were said to illustrate aspects of change essential to overcoming the poverty that breeds hunger. And all had captured international attention, for they had loosened bottlenecks that long eluded solution around the world. From Kenya's lush green highlands above the spectacular Rift Valley, my pursuit of the high performers moved westward across Africa to the drought-ridden, parched Sahel; in Asia, from the prov-ince of India where Gandhi launched his campaigns of nonviolent resistance to the Himalayan foothills in the north, from villages along Pakistan's Indus valley to the "water communities" along the Brahmaputra River in Bangladesh; in Latin America, from the rugged volcano country of central Mexico to the far western reaches of the Amazon jungle in Bolivia. The research, whose origins go back to the late 1970s, intensified in the mid-1980s, and culminated in early 1990.[4]

The effort to look more closely at exceptional performers was partly a search for more realistic expectations about the future of poverty reduction. Citizens in aid-giving countries grow weary of endless media appeals for money that will supposedly "end hunger," only to be confronted with news of persisting hardship abroad, and more appeals. Why is the process so slow? What should concerned citizens expect? The high performers had themselves taken time to mature. What were the broader implications for thinking about development? But the search was also an effort to understand which approaches to change do, in fact, succeed in helping the rural poor. What had the leaders of these strategies done to enable broad-based change to occur? It was a question that had come to interest a growing number of researchers in the 1980s.[5] As one economist put it, "What was it about the *style* of leadership that put in place the preconditions for the unsung heroes—the multitudes of rural poor for whom opportunities are usually out of reach—to step forward and take hold?"[6] Here, then, would be the focus of my journalistic lens—the leaders, the activists, their unorthodox approaches, what they had learned about getting the elusive "preconditions" right.

Rutto had himself been right to say that baffling difficulties were as much a part of the story as the progress that finally came. In many countries, those difficulties have much to do with forces "at the top," especially political and economic policies that work against rural development, stifling even the most promising of local initiatives. In the long run, overcoming the poverty that breeds hunger requires sweeping reforms in the design of national policies, as well as of global finance and trade—transformations that differ in different regions, according to local history and culture. Some of these efforts at macrolevel change I have illustrated journalistically elsewhere.[7] But beyond the improvement of top-level policies for rural growth and development, reducing hunger also involves a variety of actions that play themselves out at a very down-to-earth, practical level. This is the level at which plans and policies must be applied to the realities of rural life, and adapted over time. Here attitude and mind-set can be everything. And it is here that the best-laid plans to get the "preconditions" right easily go afield and miss the mark.

Much of the solution-defying perplexity has centered on what I came to think of, simply, as "Rutto's gap." It is a gap created by the sheer difference in culture and life-style that often exists between persons who set out to "help" the rural poor and the people who are supposed to benefit. It is a gap created by the opposing attitudes of "having" against "not having," being at the "political top" against being at the "political bottom," being "educated" against being "uneducated," "knowing what is good for people" against "being ignorant of what is needed"—and all the paternalism or subjugation that can go along with these polar states of mind. Typically the "haves" are educated urbanites trying to make policy for rural development, or locally born scientists whose training distances them from their people. Others are aid workers and donors from outside countries, people trying in one way or another to help. Changing things for the better often requires among leaders a shift of mind-set toward the rural poor, a determination to meet them "halfway," to respond to things as the poor themselves see them, to bridge the rural gap. But even the most well-meaning and well-trained practitioners have found this task more difficult and puzzling than anyone would have expected forty, or even twenty, years ago.[8]

The annals of rural development are full of cases in which the rural gap, in one form or another, defied solution and spoiled initial success. All journalists have their stories. One story from the late 1970s involved an ambitious attempt to "transfer" advanced technology. Nigeria's Ministry of Agriculture asked U.S. aid officials to help replicate America's "farm miracle" in Nigeria. The Americans confidently brought in a team of farmers from Iowa who, with the best of intentions, recommended the use of tractors and harvesting combines like those used on the Great Plains. No one realized until too late that the methods of Iowa were ill-suited to the environmental conditions of Nigeria, and the heavy machines wreaked havoc on Nigeria's thin, fragile topsoils. Importantly, the Iowan approach did not sit well with local people, especially the cultivation of vast tracts of land with a single crop. The practice outraged multitudes of small farmers who had to be moved from their land, and disrupted a centuries-old pattern of intercropping. The environmental and social disruptions could not be sustained, and the plan was abandoned.[9]

Even where efforts are made to effect change appropriate to the setting, social complexities can confound the best of plans. In Burkina Faso, one of the poorest countries of West Africa, a national program was launched to make bank credit available to small farmers and rural entrepreneurs. Backed by international aid agencies, the plan was patterned on a model that had worked in other countries, requiring people to join together in groups in order to qualify for loans. But neither the government nor the aid agencies had taken into account a critical fact: Some Burkinan communities are highly *individualistic* by tradition and would find it unacceptable to borrow in groups. They eventually refused to participate, and the program broke down.[10] Time and again in the rural development quest, history has borne out the poet William Blake's caution to the well-meaning philanthropist: "He who would do good to another must do it in Minute Particulars." And failing in the "particular" has been costly. After the 1973 famine in West Africa's Sahel, relatively little of the $13 billion in aid that poured into the region over the next decade—much of it from the pockets of private citizens in the United States and Europe— significantly reduced hunger and poverty.[11]

The exceptional performers were said to be doing better with the "details," with transcending Rutto's gap. But why had these programs achieved breakthroughs when so many other well-meaning efforts failed? As a journalist, I was not seeking pat answers or simplistic "formulas of success," but seeking rather to understand the *processes of change* these social innovators had set in motion. Specifically, I wanted to know more about three critical aspects of change that have also engaged researchers and field practitioners worldwide—aspects of *knowledge, power,* and *time.*[12] Insofar as the high-performing programs generated insights in these areas, they might also shed light on what it will take to further reduce hunger and poverty in the years ahead, and the kinds of efforts citizens in the West should support. Some aspects of these program achievements could be gleaned from news reports from abroad. But real understanding, I suspected, meant drawing closer to the changes they set in motion and to the people making those changes happen, to see things more as they themselves see them.

Note to Readers

This book is designed for both the general reader and the student of development. Information of particular interest to the specialist is placed in endnotes.

Some of the ideas and scenes are also illustrated in a public televi-

sion series, "Local Heroes, Global Change," first broadcast in the
United States in May 1990.

1. Author's interview with Dr. M. S. Swaminathan in Washington, DC, October
1987.
2. Interview with Ambassador Linowitz in Washington, DC, November 1983.
3. The selection of "exceptional performers" for a journalistic survey of this type
is bound to be somewhat arbitrary. But the selections here emerged through a consultative process based at the Harvard Institute for International Development, and
from the author's journalistic experience in covering development issues for *The
Christian Science Monitor* since the mid-1970s. The goal has been to illustrate for
students of development and for the public at large some trends of current interest to
development economists, political scientists, and anthropologists, as well as to provide a geographical spread of subjects showing the diversity of challenge confronting
development practitioners around the world.
4. For most of the development strategies highlighted here, research involved
investigation from a number of angles: preliminary research of literature from the
programs themselves and from independent analysts; in most cases, at least several
on-site visits for at least several weeks at a time; extensive interviews on location
with program leaders and with local people in remote villages; interviews on return
visits; postvisit interviews (for confirmation and reflection) with country specialists
and researchers who had long studied the programs in question—analysts based at
major research institutions in the United States, Europe, and the developing nations;
and follow-up research in professional publications. With these methods of journalistic investigation, combining direct personal observation over time with independent
opinion, the author has made an effort to overcome, albeit imperfectly, the constraints that go along with being what Robert Chambers once called a "rural tourist."
5. For instance, the survey of management approaches found in Louise G.
White's *Creating Opportunities for Change: Approaches to Managing Development
Programs* (Boulder, CO, and London: Lynne Rienner Publishers, 1987). Another attempt to draw lessons from programs widely recognized for their effectiveness is
found in Samuel Paul's *Managing Development Programs: The Lessons of Success*
(Boulder, CO: Westview Press, 1982). See also John D. Montgomery's *Bureaucrats and
People: Grassroots Participation in Third World Development* (Baltimore and London: Johns Hopkins University Press, 1988).
6. Interview with Richard Goldman at Harvard University, June 1989.
7. In the television series "Local Heroes, Global Change," a public television
presentation first broadcast in the United States in May 1990, produced by World
Development Productions, Inc., Cambridge, MA, Co-executive Producer, Richard M.
Harley; Senior Producer, Michael Camerini. See in particular the segments in Program Two ("Against the Odds") on structural adjustment of Ghana's economy (filmed
by Barbara Holocek) and aid reform in the United States (filmed by Morrow Cater),
and in Program Four ("The Global Connection"), segments on debt and trade reform
(filmed by Barbara Holocek, Morrow Cater, and Michael Camerini).
8. Of the many discussions of this subject, one of the more classic formulations is
Michael Lipton's *Why Poor People Stay Poor: Urban Bias in World Development*
(Cambridge, MA: Harvard University Press, 1976). In an insightful paper, Michael

Cernea observes that repeated failures have plagued many development programs, largely because they were "sociologically ill-informed and ill-conceived" ("Social Science Knowledge for Development Interventions," Development Discussion Paper No. 334, p. 1 [Cambridge, MA: Harvard Institute for International Development, March 1990]).

9. Recounted by Dr. Tyler Biggs of Harvard University, based on his experience heading the Ford Foundation office in Lagos, Nigeria, in the late 1970s (Interview, April 1987).

10. The individualistic worldview of the Gourmantche people of eastern Burkina Faso is strongly influenced by a concept of destiny that was described by anthropologist and linguist Dr. Richard Alan Swanson. According to this worldview, every human being has an individual destiny assigned by God following a conversation that took place before birth. The way a person's life unfolds reveals what the conversation was all about, and the divine will ("Le Destin Chez les Gourmantches," U.S.A.I.D. Contract AID/afr-C-1289, Fada N'Gourma, May 26, 1977). A discussion of the implications of the cultural sensibilities of the Gourmantche people for credit is found in Alex K. Brown, "Meeting the Needs of Voltaic Micro-Entrepreneurs: A Manual for Credit Training, Credit Administration and Management Assistance" (Washington, DC: Partnership for Productivity, 1984), pp. 5–15.

11. Different estimates are made of the exact amount. This figure was reported by the former Ford Foundation representative for East Africa, Goren Hyden, in a presentation to the Harvard Institute for International Development, February 5, 1986. The comments of several other students of agricultural development in the Sahel also are instructive: "In spite of relatively large investments in national and international agricultural research and in specific agricultural development programs there, agriculture has continued to stagnate in these countries and there has been little diffusion of new cereal cultivars" (John H. Sanders, Joseph G. Nagy, and Sunder Ramaswamy, "Developing New Agricultural Technologies for the Sahelian Countries: The Burkina Faso Case," in *Economic Development and Cultural Change*, Vol. 39, October 1990, No. 1, p. 1).

12. By *knowledge* I refer to the fundamental assumptions that drive plans for change and the transfer of technology; by *power*, to the political context in which change must occur; and by *time*, to concerns over the term allowed for change to occur. These three aspects of change illuminate the structure of this book as shown in the table of contents.

PART ONE

Shifting Assumptions:
Whose Ways Are Best?

Experienced Scientist
Meets Experienced Peasant

PUEBLA, MEXICO

Plan Puebla is one of the classic experiments in spreading new technologies to the rural poor. Its predecessor, the "Green Revolution," had brought spectacular increases in wheat production to Mexico in the 1950s and 1960s but benefited only a minority of farmers possessing large landholdings and good irrigation. In the late 1960s, a second generation of Green Revolution agronomists began an experiment to reach the worse-off majority, small farmers whose mainstay was not wheat, but corn. Many in the scientific community doubted the willingness, or ability, of these farmers to adopt new technologies. By the 1980s, the agronomists' assumptions about poor illiterate farmers, and what it takes to share "scientific methods" with them, had totally changed.

Few in 1976 could have anticipated the program's collapse. Never before had the small farmers of central Mexico been doing so well. These were the beneficiaries of new efforts by agronomists to spread high-yielding corn seeds and improved growing methods—Green Revolution technologies—to the rural poor.[1] And the response of peasant farmers seemed to be proving wrong the skeptics who doubted their receptivity to change. *Campesinos* were adopting new farming techniques as rapidly as had rich farmers in the north of Mexico, and to great advantage. East of Mexico City, in the state of Puebla, corn yields were up more than 40 percent since the experiment began just ten years before.[2] Farmer participation had climbed from 30 families to 9,000—nearly one third of all farm families in the state. The experiment, now known as "Plan Puebla," was attracting national and international attention. The government, with help from international donors, decided to replicate the Puebla model in fifteen other states. And to back up activities in the field, a new research center, CEICADAR, was being built near Mexico City.[3]

But the momentum of change suddenly turned for the worse. Increases in corn production leveled off despite the fact that even higher increases were within easy reach. Farmers getting yields of 2.6 tons per hectare could have been raising their production to 3.2, but were not going for it. Many were opting for less than 2.6. Their participation in bank credit programs for the purchase of fertilizer began to fall off.[4] Also, production of corn fell relative to other crops. In six short years, from 1976 to 1982, the rising statistics of success dropped like a stock market crash, returning to levels not much higher than they were at the start. Scientists at CEICADAR found it difficult not to admit failure. Still more difficult was understanding why the promise so suddenly turned sour.

In time, they did understand. When I first visited the scientists of Plan Puebla in the late 1970s and again in the early 1980s, they were not all sure what the decline meant, or where it would lead. By the time I connected with them again in the late 1980s, they had no doubt.

■

Alfonso Macias had arranged for a journey to Huezotzingo. In that remote rural locale, a team of Mexican agronomists and social scientists was gathering lessons of the past to focus agendas for the future. "You need to see Huezotzingo in order to understand where we've been and where we're going," Macias explained. Our Land-Rover pushed out from the research center at CEICADAR and headed east into the state of Puebla. At 7,000 feet, the morning air was chill but invigorating. Rays from the rising sun caught the summit of Pico de Orizaba, a blue-green volcano capped in snow. To the north a cluster of clouds dispersed, revealing the peaks of two more volcanoes. "The people have names for these," said Macias. "One is known as the Sleeping Lady, the other they call One Who Watches Over Her." Macias's English was fluent yet retained all the warm, melodic undu-

Agronomist Alfonso Macias (right) and farmer

lations of Mexican Spanish. He was one of the second-generation Green Revolution scientists whose idealism was bred during the euphoric years of the first revolution. In his brown corduroys, red T-shirt, and blue nylon jacket, he might have passed for any clean-cut young Mexican, except for some small gold letters on his jacket that read IOWA STATE. Graduate study in the United States was common among the Plan Puebla agronomists, and Macias was no exception.[5] "After you live in an American university town," he said, "it's not exactly easy to think of coming back to work here among the rural poor, especially when you know you'll have to support your wife on a starting salary of $6,000. We decided to return, at least for now."

Across the landscape, timeless remnants of Mexican village life started to come into view. Stucco homes were awash with color. The steeples and painted domes of flat-faced, slit-windowed brick chapels reached for heaven. Road signs still carried the names of ancient towns that had long since yielded to European domination, though not to extermination—Zacaloacayan, Tlalancaleca, Amozoc, Tecuanipan. Huge earthen mounds, once the foundations of Aztec temples, now bore churches plated on the inside with Indian gold. Modernity, not to be denied, had contributed adornments of its own to the countryside. A Volkswagen plant sprawled conspicuously on the outskirts of the state's main city. Billboards advertised American tractors, Coke, and Pepsi. At a crossroads, petrol stations sported gleaming gas pumps under festive canopies—shining but grim reminders that the oil wealth on which Mexico once based her hopes had been squandered by poor management, corruption, and the unkind exigencies of shifting world prices.

Plan Puebla's scientists had targeted their efforts toward an area encompassing 50,000 farm families, descendants of peasants who first gained title to their land in the decades following the Revolution of 1911 when huge haciendas were eventually divided and redistributed to the poor.[6] Most plots measured only two and a half hectares, a little over six acres. Plots were often divided further into five or six sectors to accommodate different crops or to be managed by other family members. Land reform had given campesinos a source of income security they had not known before. But the breakup of lands had also blocked the kind of economy of scale that made corn farming so profitable in the American midwest.[7]

"In the early days of Plan Puebla," explained Macias, "our researchers came up with what seemed the ideal combination of hybrid seed, fertilizer, and plant spacing for these fields.[8] We also arranged for better bank credit and insurance for small farmers.[9] Unfortunately our seeds got abandoned by many campesinos because local varieties often did better. But the fertilizer and cropping recommendations were accepted, and paid off handsomely. Production soared. Obviously we were very encouraged. That's why it was so hard to accept the downturn that came in 1976. Why were the campesinos rejecting goals we knew they could reach? We began to ask ourselves if campesinos were simply not as *rational* as we had once thought."

Plan Puebla agronomists were well aware of international research about "peasant rationality." In a departure from the old colonialist view of peasants as lazy, backward, and irrational,[10] a growing number of economists in the mid-1960s argued that most peasant farmers are, in fact, industrious and economically quite rational. To be sure, they conceded, peasants are poor. But this is no proof that they are irrational or inefficient. They simply have too little access to the fertilizers and seeds needed to do better. Offer the choice of a more productive and profitable way to farm, and the campesino will, more often than not, seize the opportunity.[11] By the early 1970s, however, other researchers were arguing that the way peasants reason is not so predictably rational after all. Farmers do not always opt for maximum profits, they said. Fear of risk often overrides their entrepreneurial instinct to invest. Social goals can also outweigh the profit motive—a desire for leisure, activities that bring status or fulfill community obligations, even altruistic deeds with no prospect of pay.[12] Still, if peasant farmers were not always rational in Western terms, by the mid-1970s it was no longer possible for researchers to believe they were "naturally backward" or "resistant to change."[13] What baffled Plan Puebla agronomists was the fact that Puebla's rational farmers seemed to be reducing corn production at a time when new gains could be made easily, and at very little cost.

"Our first glimmer of understanding came in 1976," said Alfonso Macias, shouting to be heard over the Land-Rover's engine. "A new study showed that our farmers were making much more income doing odd jobs *off* the farm than we had realized. This was a shock. It suggested that our own goal of increasing corn yields—not the farmers' irrationality—might be at fault. By driving so hard for increasing yields, we scientists might be working against farmer interests, for the campesinos could earn more money if their time was not all tied down on the farm."[14] Macias paused and looked toward the road ahead. "Another shock came when our chief researcher—Antonio Turrent—traveled to India. But this is a story I want you to hear from Turrent himself. He heads up our research efforts here in the *campos.*"

■

Turrent's research camp looked more like a country warehouse than an outpost for scientific research. The choice to locate in this remote area was typical of the Plan Puebla philosophy to move research out to where farmers live, rather than confining it to central laboratories and exporting the results. Turrent was waiting for us in a spacious, sunlit room, talking with younger colleagues next to a chalkboard.

Antonio Turrent

He, too, had received his scientific training at Iowa State University, though he was more senior than Alfonso Macias. In appearance, Turrent had the look of actor Robert Conrad. His square face and chin, rectangular wire-rims, and ruddy complexion were set off by a white turtleneck sweater that rose from the collar of an open-necked blue fieldshirt. "India?" he said, "yes, that *was* a turning point in our understanding of small farmers and how we should be working with them." The terse, measured bursts of his voice carried scientific authority, but his speech was warmed by the congeniality shared by most of his Mexican colleagues. "When I went to India," he said, "it was 1978. Of course, their farmers had many similarities to our own. Many work under similar conditions—rainfed water supply, not irrigation, great economic insecurities, and so on. To my surprise, however, many Indian farmers were getting far greater yields and income *out of the same inputs*. That got us thinking: What is it that makes a

8

small peasant farm work, and what makes one work better than another?" He grinned, picked up a piece of chalk, and began to draw.

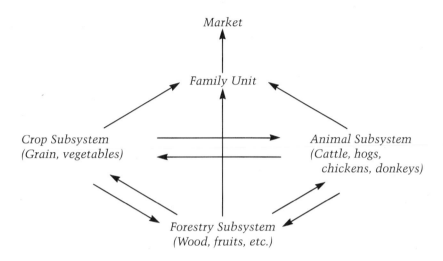

"Here you see a simplified outline of the parts of a small farm, whether in India or Mexico, or most anywhere. There are three main subsystems—crops, animals, and forestry. And they each depend to some extent on the others. I am drawing arrows in two directions between the subsystems to show how there are ways of linking the subsystems for mutual benefit. For instance, the cropping subsystem can benefit from energy and manure that come from the animal subsystem, while the animal subsystem can benefit from crop stalks that make good animal feed, and so on. What distinguished the Indian farms was the fact that farmers were finding all kinds of new ways to enhance these linkages. From the cropping subsystem they were taking cut plant stalks and mixing them with chicken droppings to improve the nutrition of cattle feed, at no extra cost. They found their tree subsystem could benefit from soil nutrients that come from certain cropping patterns. You get the point—Indian farmers were getting a lot more out of the links between animal, fruit, and cropping subsystems. Seeing this, we began to understand much more clearly how peasants think about their farms. They're really *systems* thinkers. When they want to improve their farms, they want to see what will make the *whole system* work better, not just any one part."

Turrent seemed to delight at the thought of this discovery, though it had come, back then, at some considerable emotional cost. In 1978 he and his colleagues had been striving for more than a decade to improve one crop in one subsystem—corn. They had failed to see the importance Mexican farmers attached to fruit, cattle, and employment off the farm. Farmers rejected "scientific plans" that aimed for the highest corn yields because that would mean sinking too much investment in one subsystem at the expense of the others. As a scientific enterprise, Plan Puebla needed not just a minor adjustment in its approach, but a complete overhaul.

"Looking back now," said Turrent, "the need to see campesinos differently and to approach research differently seems utterly obvious. But when you're in the middle of a campaign, driving for a goal you think is within reach, you can't always see straight.[15] Fortunately we were able to understand. Now we're working on a new prototype for research. You must see it in the field. But not until you've had a chance to see Heliodoro Diaz. He's the one who gave us proof we were really on the right track."

∎

Agronomists trained in predictable science are often tempted to separate their "pure research" on the research station from the unpredictabilities of social reality. Not a few of Plan Puebla's agronomists had tried to resist this temptation.[16] One was Heliodoro Diaz. In fact, he rejected the separation altogether. Diaz was a new kind of "human hybrid" generated by the Green Revolution—the agronomist cum social scientist. His early career had followed the normal pattern of Plan Puebla scientists—completing advanced agronomic study in Mexico, then helping to launch Plan Puebla in the field. But Diaz then abandoned convention and headed for the University of Wisconsin to study rural sociology. Scientific research, he believed, would not really meet the needs of the rural poor until agronomists grasped the social and economic forces affecting rural poverty as campesinos themselves perceive them. In the person of Diaz and in other agrosociologists, physical science would condescend to partnership with social science, and hold its breath to see if the crossbreed would bear fruit.

John Scheck

Diaz himself cut the image of a charismatic college professor—tall, dark, bearded, handsome, reflective. Though he was in his early 50s, his beard had not turned altogether gray. The informality of his green designer jeans and matching pullover jacket showed that years had not distanced him from the younger generation. It was Diaz's study of the way farmers respond to drought that attracted greatest attention at the research center. "Our results seemed, at first, exactly what you would expect," he said, walking through gardens outside CEICADAR. "During times of drought, campesinos tried to protect their flow of income by shifting away from crops to fruit and animals. They also spent more time working off the farm."[17] He paused to stroke his long beard. "But you know, the closer we looked at what was happening, the more we began to realize just how *sophisticated* a game the farmers play to protect themselves against hard times. They not only manage complex interlinked farming systems; they deliberately keep their assets spread out so they will not be too dependent on any one aspect of the system. If any one investment fails, they fall back on another to ensure at least some income. In other words, like most of us, they do not put all their eggs in one basket. It became utterly clear that we could never succeed by pushing a single goal like maximizing corn. If we scientists were going to really help, we would have to look for ways to improve their *whole* systems. That's the road we finally took."

■

Turrent's experimental "prototype" was an attempt to align research with the new understanding of peasant thinking. Trials had begun on a farm not far from the station at Huezotzingo. There, on a small tract of land, a farmer named Juan Montes was trying to make ends meet for his wife and eight children. Farming conditions were typical of the region: Farmers had to contend with seven different types of soil composed of seven very different combinations of minerals and organic matter. Agronomists roamed the area with soil charts that looked like complex contour maps colored according to some paint-by-the-numbers scheme. Rainfall was scarce and irregular, making each year's crop yields unpredictable at best. Hail was common in August and September, frost from October to March. The winter months saw little water at all.

Waiting at the household gate were Montes's wife, mother, and son. The two women wore their jet-black hair in long braids and had angular features that were unmistakably Aztec. Conspicuous by his absence, Montes himself was working at a part-time job in a nearby town—one of the many "eggs" in the family's economic basket. Alfonso Macias unzipped his Iowa State jacket and led the way into a small open-air courtyard, surrounded on two sides with bi-level structures that housed a kitchen and living quarters. The aroma of freshly cooked tortillas wafted through the courtyard, occasionally overpowered by the smell of cows, goats, and chickens kept in a makeshift shelter adjoining the house. Twenty paces beyond the shelter were fields densely cultivated with fruit trees, corn stalks, beans, and leafy ground vegetables, all planted in no apparent order. "This may look disordered to the uneducated eye," said Alfonso Macias. "But actually it's quite orderly, if you see it as the farmer does." He grinned. "Crops are mingled, but there's a logic to it."

Montes's logic was based partly on intercepting every ray of sun with green vegetable matter, leaving not a single square millimeter of ground exposed. Complex intercropping was the result. Antonio Turrent had originally returned to Puebla from Iowa State with hopes of reversing the pattern, opening up vast stretches of country-side for corn alone, to be harvested with huge combines like those used in America's midwest. "But there's no way you can use com-bines to harvest fields that are intercropped like this," explained Macias. "And we learned that it's really not possible to get the people to stop intercropping. They've long believed it has benefits—more variety of crops, better nutrition. They've convinced *us* of that, too. We're starting to listen."[18]

Coming to understand the views of farmers, in addition to the costs and benefits of traditional methods, agronomists also began to discover new research directions, particularly for improving the links between subsystems. Macias pointed to a corner of the Montes farm where new ways had been found to grind up roughage—corn stalks and weeds—from the cropping system and mix it with mo-lasses and chicken droppings to produce a far more nutritious feed for the animals, at very little extra cost. In another corner, new methods of fruit preservation were being tested. In an outdoor shel-ter, Macias pulled out screen-bottomed drawers from a tall wooden chest in which slices of apple and other fruits were drying for mar-ket. Meanwhile, specialists brought in to study the tree and fruit subsystem had identified a boron mineral deficiency that was caus-ing the fruit of pear trees to crack, making them unfit for market. Once the lack was corrected, farmer Montes and his neighbors were able to reopen a market that had collapsed. "There are all kinds of ways research can increase efficiencies and improve marketing possi-bilities," said Alfonso Macias. "And once you start to see the impli-cations for improving incomes out here, you see why the stakes are high in understanding the farmer as the systems thinker and risk-manager he really is."

It was premature to judge whether Turrent's prototype would sur-vive the test of time. But Macias, for one, was certain that the reason-ing behind it would persist, expressed in one form of research or another. "You know, Dr. Turrent said it well. When you first work here in the campos, he said, everything seems so mixed up. If you're trained to be an expert in one crop, you end up seeing nothing the way farmers themselves see it. You may push for an isolated idea they won't accept. Then you try to look at things in the integrated way farmers do, and you begin to get a bit scared, for you realize that they know many things. But you realize if you want to help them, you have to listen. Then suddenly the listening surfaces an idea that you had never thought of before. You realize it has a real chance to work. And that's what you want to know more than anything else. As an agronomist you want to know that, when all is said and done, you really *did* make some contribution, that you were not entirely wrong, that your research had some real chance to be used. It's only through these partnerships with farmers that we've really been able to tell."[19]

1. Commitment by the Mexican government to spread improved technologies for farming corn—the peasant's staple—came much more slowly than for wheat. Between 1943 and 1963 the introduction of Green Revolution methods for wheat boosted production from an average 8 to 15 bushels per acre to between 50 and 88 bushels per acre. These methods involved the use of high-yielding seeds coupled with plant spacing methods, fertilizer, and irrigation. While increases came in the traditional wheat-growing areas of central and northern Mexico, gains were also outstanding on large farms in the Pacific northwest, whose share of national wheat production increased from marginal in the 1940s to nearly two-thirds of total production in the 1960s (E. C. Stakman, Richard Bradfield, & Paul C. Mangelsdorf, *Campaigns Against Hunger* [Cambridge, MA: Belknap Press of Harvard University Press, 1967], pp. 90–91).

Advances in corn production, in contrast, got off the ground slowly. The first new corn varieties were actually released in 1949, not long after the first new wheats. But by 1960, well after the new wheats had taken over virtually all Mexican wheat lands, the agricultural census showed that less than one-twentieth of the maize lands were planted to hybrid corn (see Michael Redclift, "Production Programs for Small Farmers: Plan Puebla as Myth and Reality," in *Economic Development and Cultural Change*, 1983, 31 (3), footnote 5, p. 567). Partly, national agricultural policies gave priority to wheat farmers operating larger farms in well-irrigated zones. More generally, national policies, whether in wheat or corn, tended to favor better-off farmers, to the disadvantage of smallholders, most of whom grow corn. Often the high-yielding seeds, fertilizers, and other farm inputs, produced and distributed through state-owned agencies, were made available at subsidized prices only to farmers who already had advantages such as the credit to make purchases, the means to pay for shipping services, access to major roads, or an existing status as clients of government research and extension services (Merilee Grindle, *State and Countryside: Development Policy and Agrarian Politics in Latin America* [Baltimore & London: Johns Hopkins University Press, 1988], pp. 60–61).

2. Some studies show that maize yields had increased between 0.58 and 1.35 tons per hectare from 1967 to 1976, with 97 percent of those using the new technologies experiencing benefit. However, not all adopted the "package" of recommendations equally—17 percent used fertilizer to a high degree, 63 percent to a medium degree, 17 percent very little, and 3 percent relied on traditional practices (Interview, July 1989, with Leobardo Jimenez, Director Plan Puebla, Colegio de Postgraduados at Chapingo, Mexico).

3. CEICADAR is the acronym for Centro de Ensenanza, Investigacion y Capacitacion para el Desarrollo Agricola Regional.

4. From 18 percent to 10 percent (Interview, August 1987, with Heliodoro Diaz-Cisneros, Colegio de Postgraduados at Chapingo, Mexico).

5. The development of such "human capital" has been critically important in countries where agricultural development has made major strides. See Uma Lele & Arthur A. Goldsmith, "The Development of National Agricultural Research Capacity: India's Experience with the Rockefeller Foundation and Its Significance for Africa" (Washington, DC: The World Bank Development Research Department discussion paper, August 15, 1987).

6. As Merilee Grindle (op. cit., pp. 41–42, 62–67) notes, Mexican national policy and rhetoric concerning small-farmer rights has fluctuated greatly in the twentieth century. While the 1917 Constitution promised massive agrarian reform, land was not actually redistributed until the administration of Lazaro Cardenas in 1934. Between 1934 and 1940 over 20 million hectares of land were distributed—about two times as much as in the preceding twenty years. Some of the land went to individual farm families and some to communal holdings known as *ejidos* involving parcels granted to towns, which in turn distributed them among members to be worked either individually or communally. (This redistribution, which by 1940 had left half Mexico's cultivated land in the hands of ejidos, sharply contrasted with the pattern of land concentration in other parts of Latin America from 1850 to 1930. The general trend outside Mexico, according to Grindle, had been decidedly anti-smallholder, tending toward consolidation into large estates whose owners sought to monopolize resources and labor so as to benefit from the growing export economy.) Despite Mexico's land reform of the 1930s and state policies making resources available to ejidos, national policy again shifted between 1940 and 1970 in favor of industrialization and larger farmers. The Echeverria administration, from 1970 to 1976, brought still another policy shift back in favor of increased investment in agricultural development (concurrent with the flowering of Plan Puebla). The subsequent administration of Lopez Portillo veered away from the small farmer, opening relatively more opportunities to larger ones.

7. Even where collective farming did create larger farms in parts of central Mexico, American-style single-crop strategies were frustrated by the sheer variability of soil conditions.

8. Specifically, the goal was to rapidly increase maize production among small farmers who produce for subsistence with traditional methods, without extensive investment in irrigation or other methods of countering climatic adversities (Centro Internacional de Mejoramiento de Maiz y Trigo [CIMMYT], "The Puebla Project: Seven Years of Experience from 1967–1973" [El Batan, Mexico: CIMMYT, 1974]). The initial technological package included a combination of hybrid maize seeds, fertilizer, credit, farmer education, and institutional coordination. Actually, the seed component of Plan Puebla's technological "package" proved a disappointment. Hybrid seeds—developed at scientific research stations—were often outperformed in the field by local native varieties. Ultimately, Plan Puebla agronomists dropped the seed component of the program altogether and concentrated on fertilizer recommendations (130 kilograms of nitrogen, 40 kilograms of potassium P205) and spacing of plants (Interview, September 1987, with Heliodoro Diaz-Cisneros).

9. Banks would not give loans to purchase fertilizer or seed without insurance policies in place. One of Plan Puebla's main innovations was coordinating such insurance services and credit with other government-run farm-input programs. While

some coordination efforts had been made in the past, major problems were evident by the mid-1960s. In particular, the agricultural extension service was fundamentally separate from the research institutions (E. C. Stakman et al., op. cit., pp. 205–206). Plan Puebla planners believed that political conditions had become particularly favorable for redressing the coordination problem. Their plan included a feedback system to circulate information between researchers, field workers, and government credit and extension services, to ensure that all conditions were right for small farmers to succeed.

10. In Kenya's colonial days, for instance, some British authorities believed that peasant farmers would not respond to price incentives and that only European farmers could supply enough food for the African labor force (John Gerhart, "The Diffusion of Hybrid Maize in Western Kenya" [Mexico City: CIMMYT, 1975], p. 14).

11. Such conclusions attracted interest in the 1960s not just for their novelty; they also dispelled the nagging doubts of international donors about whether to put new technologies in the hands of peasants. Many researchers now said yes. Some of the landmark studies of the "poor but efficient" hypothesis that indicate the technological efficiency of small farmers include W. D. Hopper, "Allocation Efficiency in Traditional Indian Agriculture," *Journal of Farm Economics*, 1965, 47 (3); T. W. Schultz, *Transforming Traditional Agriculture* (New Haven: Yale University Press, 1964); and P. A. Yotopoulos & J. B. Nugent, *Economics of Development* (New York: Harper & Row, 1976). These theories tended to argue that small farmers generally maximize their profits up to the limit of available resources and technologies. A good overview of the "poor but efficient" hypothesis, criticisms, and subsequent adjustments in the theory is included in Subrata Ghatak & Ken Ingersent, *Agriculture and Economic Development* (Baltimore: Johns Hopkins University Press, 1984), ch. 6. Some observations from this overview are included in notes that follow.

12. Several types of studies called into question, or at least seriously qualified, the image of peasant farmers as "economically rational persons" attempting above all to "maximize profits." The studies resulted in a more complicated and varied picture. Some indicated, on the one hand, that a farmer's desire to reduce risk—to ensure stability of output and income, and avoid short-run losses—could take precedence over strictly rational profit maximization (M. Lipton, "The Theory of the Optimising Peasant," *Journal of Development Studies*, 1968, 4(3); M. Schulter & T. Mount, "Management Objectives of the Peasant Farmer: An Analysis of Risk Aversion in the Choice of Cropping Pattern, Surat District, India," [Ithaca, NY: Cornell University Department of Agricultural Economics, Occasional Paper No. 78, 1974]; J. M. Wolgin, "Resource Allocation and Risk: A Case Study of Smallholder Agriculture in Kenya," *American Journal of Agricultural Economics*, 1975, 54(4)). Some studies, on the other hand, showed that, contrary to the "poor but efficient" hypothesis, the scope of peasant agriculture allows the improvement of farm productivity and incomes by persuading farmers to make simple improvements in crop management practices (K. Shapiro, "Efficiency Differentials in Peasant Agriculture and Their Implications for Development Policies," in *Contributed Papers Read at the 16th International Conference of Agricultural Economics* [Oxford: Institute of Agricultural Economics, 1977]; *World Development Report* [Washington, DC: World Bank, 1981], pp. 39–40). Still other studies provided evidence that not all poor farmers are averse to risk. Some in the Philippines, for instance, gambled on cash-intensive practices in the hope that quick payoffs would get them out of debt (J. Roumasset, *Rice and Risk* [Amsterdam: North-Holland, 1976]).

13. In their overview of the impact of Green Revolution technologies, Per Pinstrup-

Andersen and Peter B. R. Hazell confirmed that farmers "have widely adopted high-yielding wheat and rice varieties irrespective of farm size and tenurial status. In many regions suited for the high-yielding varieties, low-income farmers have adopted them to at least the same extent as larger farmers, and the most recent studies suggest that net gains per unit of land tend to be larger on smaller farms" (P. Pinstrup-Andersen & P. B. R. Hazell, "The Impact of the Green Revolution and Prospects for the Future," in M. Price Gittinger et al., eds., *Food Policy: Integrating Supply, Distribution, and Consumption* [Baltimore & London: Johns Hopkins University Press, 1987], pp. 106–118).

14. Manuel Villa Issa, *El Mercado de Trabajo y la Adopcion de Technologia Nueva de Producion Agricola: El Caso del Plan Puebla* (Chapingo, Mexico: Colegio de Postgraduados, 1977).

15. In the late 1970s and early 1980s, experts in rural sociology were increasingly critical of the biases agricultural scientists carried with them in their work in the countryside. Robert Chambers, for one, observed that "Agricultural literature is replete with books and papers that treat production as though it were a sole and adequate objective. . . . It is difficult for some scientists to accept that they have anything to learn from rural people, or to recognize that there is a parallel system of knowledge to their own, which is complementary, usually valid, and in some respects superior. . . . And even when, as increasingly occurs, scientists do seek to learn from farmers, they are still conditioned to imposing their own categories, meanings, and priorities, rather than learning from and thinking with those farmers" (R. Chambers, "Understanding Professionals: Small Farmers and Scientists" [New York: International Agricultural Development Service, 1980], pp. 2–3).

16. Central leadership for blending the concerns of social reality with the planning of agronomic research should be credited largely to Leobardo Jimenez, director of CEICADAR.

17. In a normal year farm families earned about 50 percent of their income from crops, 25 percent from animal husbandry, 17 percent from fruit production, and 8 percent from other activities. In drought years the income from crops fell drastically to 18 percent; that derived from animal husbandry and fruit production rose to 35 percent and 25 percent, respectively. The relation of on-farm to off-farm income also shifted sharply. In a normal year like 1970 the farmers on Plan Puebla's credit list were getting 68 percent of their income from on-farm production, 32 percent from off-farm employment. In drought years, on-farm income dropped to 42 percent; off-farm income rose to 57 percent (Interview, September 1987, with Heliodoro Diaz-Cisneros).

18. In the early days of Plan Puebla, farmers were urged to stop their common practice of mixing other vegetables with their corn, and to monocrop. Despite repeated pressure from scientists and repeated assurances by farmers that they would comply, many farmers continued to interplant beans with the corn. When agronomists returned to farmers' fields to see how crops were progressing, they would find bean plants growing up the corn stalks. Farmers explained that their families simply *liked* beans and that intercropping actually increased production per acre. In 1971 research chief Turrent decided to scientifically test the farmers' assertion. A year later his study showed that intercropping reduced maize yield by one ton per hectare but also yielded one ton of beans per hectare on the same land. Per unit measure the beans brought farmers two times as much income as corn and provided twice the protein.

19. In the late 1980s Antonio Turrent was appointed head of INIFAP, the national agricultural research institute of the Mexican government; Alfonso Macias became dirctor of CEICADAR.

2

A Race between Food and Population: Science Meets Social Change

KAKAMEGA, KENYA

Small farms in the highlands of western Kenya benefited from some of the same technologies that helped the corn farmers of Mexico. But social change swept the highlands, and technologies that had won over the people in some communities lost favor almost overnight. To keep abreast of change, Kenya's agricultural researchers had to go back to the drawing board.

From Central America, travel nine thousand miles east along the Equator and, nearly half a world from the cornfields of Mexico, you reach the highlands of western Kenya, the largest corn-growing region on the African continent. The highlands are surrounded by some of the most fabled and visually breathtaking topography: to the southwest, the marshy banks of Lake Victoria, second largest freshwater lake in the world; to the southeast, the cedar forests of the Mau Escarpment. Not far from there, the famed aviatrix and horse trainer Beryl Markham flew some of the first flights across uncharted wilderness, and Baroness Karen Blixen came with her husband from Denmark to farm coffee, later writing about it under the pen name Isak Dinesen.[1] Eastward the earth drops some 4,000 feet from its plateau at 9,000 feet to the Rift Valley floor, only to rise again to 17,000-foot Mt. Kenya, where actor William Holden built his lodge and nature preserve. To the north, the highlands rise once more to 14,000-foot Mt. Elgon, not far from the site of the Mau Mau rebellion that helped to free Kenya from British rule in 1963. And to the west, the land descends into vast stretches of agriculturally rich Uganda, which could be—were it not for intertribal and political strife—some of the most productive farmland in all of Africa.

But it was not the *surrounds* of Kenya's highlands that interested the agriculturalists of Mexico; they were intrigued by developments in the highlands themselves. The early encounters of Mexican and Kenyan agriculture came in the 1950s when a delegation of Kenyan corn-seed breeders visited Central America looking for new strains from the seed banks of Mexico and Colombia. Cross-breeding the Mexican strains with their own seeds back in Africa, they produced corn hybrids with spectacularly higher yields. Agronomists in Mexico, working on their own corn revolution, watched from afar as a parallel story played itself out across Kenya's highlands. Use of the new seeds rapidly swept the Kenyan countryside. They first took hold on larger farms owned by families of European background, descendants of the settlers who first brought corn farming to Kenya at the turn of the century, but were as rapidly accepted on small farms worked by indigenous African farmers. Once again, if some in the industrialized world questioned the ability of illiterate peasants to apply new technologies, Kenya's farmers left no doubt. They picked up the hybrid seeds faster than did farmers in Iowa during the 1930s and 1940s.[2] The rapidity of change was due partly to the sheer performance of the new seeds and partly to a shrewd marketing decision by the breeders. The breeders adapted to their purpose the highly successful method used by Wilkinson Sword to make Wilkinson's the people's shaving blade of choice: selling through small mom-and-pop shops. As with blades, so with seeds: Breeders persuaded stores to carry their innovative product, word got out, and rich and poor farmers alike began to sing the praises of the Amerafrican cross.[3]

Yet Kenya's technological change became radically disrupted in ways that Mexico's had never been. In the Mexican state of Puebla, social conditions had stayed relatively stable. Researchers had reasonable certainty that the new methods they developed would remain useful, and be used, over time. Kenya's highlands, by contrast, experienced sweeping social changes that, in some areas, drastically altered the technology equation. In the late 1970s people began moving into the fertile highlands at an alarming rate. Migration had begun, more slowly, well before independence in 1963 but accelerated when land reforms after independence encouraged the transfer of land from Europeans to Africans. Meanwhile, birth rates soared. With increasing population density, more of the better farmland was desired by more and more people. On average, families in the highlands were having eight children—one of the highest rates of growth in the world. In some areas population density reached 600 persons per square kilometer and continued to grow, raising fears of land abuse, soil degradation, and possible food shortages on a mass scale.[4] One effect of the new demographics was soon clear: Families were dividing the land among their sons, making the average farm size smaller and smaller. But by the early 1980s, the eventual effect of population change on living standards was anybody's guess. At stake was the solvability of a problem far more common to development planners in Asia than Africa: how to feed rapidly increasing numbers of people who must live on smaller and smaller plots.

One response came from agriculturalists at CIMMYT, Mexico's International Maize and Wheat Improvement Center. They did not pretend to know what should be done but were convinced that social changes in the highlands must be better understood if technologies were to keep pace with changing needs. In the mid-1970s CIMMYT launched a series of efforts to teach farming systems survey methods in countries of East Africa, including Kenya. By the time I arrived in Nairobi nearly a decade later, a generation of agricultural researchers had been trained.[5] I rented a car and headed for the highlands to see what, if any, had been the results.

■

The Ngong Road leads northwest out of Nairobi across the half-farmed, half-forested Ngong Hills. An afternoon's drive beyond the hills, I was told, lay Kakamega, the highland district where social change was most pronounced. In Kakamega, population density had already reached an astonishing 700 persons per square kilometer. New growth threatened to outrun anything researchers could do to make food production keep pace, or to care for the land.

Between the Ngong Hills and the highlands lay the great Rift Valley, part of the massive geological fault that cuts all the way from Malawi in southern Africa up through Egypt and Israel to the Dead Sea. A traveler journeying by car across the Valley sees not a hint of the population crisis on the highlands beyond the Valley. Tree-sparse savannah stretches as far as the eye can see, broken only by the occasional Masai village or wandering herdsman. From the ridge of the Ngong Hills, Karen Blixen spent long hours gazing across these plains. Rivaling the staid, still beauty of the plains below is the boisterous, shifting theater of clouds in the sky above. The blue of Kenyan skies has a quality that seems, at times, touchable—more liquid than air. It is a tangibility that makes even the farthest horizon seem intimately near. Burgeoning puffs of white clouds make brash but beautiful entries across the azure sky—as Karen Blixen put it, "a profusion of mighty, weightless, ever-changing clouds towering up and sailing in it."[6]

As I crossed the Rift, I was still trying to decide what to make of two experts I had interviewed the day before—one an economist, the other an ecologist. Each had been analyzing trends in the highlands, with utterly different conclusions. Malcolm Hall was the alarmist. A Harvard agricultural economist, he was working in Nairobi for the Kenyan Ministry of Agriculture. "You have to see these changes in perspective," he said. "Here you have a situation in which only a few generations ago, most Kenyans were earning their keep as herdsmen—and with lots of space to do it in. Now they are farmers, and the concentration of people on the more fertile lands is coming about faster than anywhere on earth. Each year there are a million more Kenyans. They'll have to live off land that is *not* expanding, farming much of it with intensive methods like the Asians use. But Kenya does not start out with the advantages you had in India, Indonesia, or China. There people had generations of experience with intensive farming. Here we've got the poulation density of Asia without the initial advantages. The question is, Can we find a more intensive agriculture that will not destroy the land, and can we do it in time to deal with the demands of population?"

While Hall was sounding the alarm, ecologist Mike Norton-Griffiths was testing a more optimistic hypothesis.[7] The population trend could actually be an advantage, he suspected, not a liability. Norton-Griffiths had devised a research technique for determining the effects of population growth on land upkeep in the highlands of western Kenya. In a single-engine aircraft he flew hundreds of low-level flights above the area, doing sample surveys of land-use patterns. Translating the photographs into computer data, he compared them with government records of past land use and began to reach conclusions that confounded even his own expectations. "People assume that an increase in population must mean stripping these fertile lands of trees and overgrazing them with cattle," he said, bending over computer printouts strewn across his office desk at Ecosystems, Ltd. "Our own data are showing the reverse. As land use intensifies in the highlands, we're seeing *improvement* in people's upkeep of the land."

It was, in Norton-Griffiths's terms, a tender-loving-care effect. "If you have only a small plot," he explained, "each plant must be nurtured, its leaves examined every day, the animals cared for in stalls rather than pasture. Trees are kept, or planted, for shade and fruit. Our photographs show that where there's an increase in population density, the planting of trees is actually *increasing.* Trees are forcing themselves *back into the system*, not being stripped from it." For all the alarm over population density, Norton-Griffiths argued that only a small amount of land in the highlands was yet reaching its full productive potential—three out of every ten acres. By improving farm techniques, he believed, crop yields could jump another 60 percent. "I'm one of the few who believe that Kenya's population must rise from the current 25 million to 100 million before the country will scratch the surface of its cropping potential."[8]

Norton-Griffiths had a point, though time would have to pass for history's verdict to come in. Across the Rift Valley the road climbed steadily into the highlands, meandering through hills blanketed for miles with close-cropped, meticulously trimmed tea bushes. The air cooled. A sign appeared at the roadside: "You are now crossing the Equator." The earth began to get visibly rocky. Pebbles turned into stones, stones into rocks, and rocks into huge glacial boulders that sat proudly astride the landscape like enthroned royalty. Thatched huts intermingled with boulders and trees in a symbiosis seemingly ordained by some primeval Ice-age hand. A town approached, and another sign: "You are entering Kakamega, the Lions Club Welcomes You." There followed a long series of flat-roofed shops and fruit stands on both sides of the street. It was here, in the southern part of the Kakamega district that the agronomist named Jeremiah Rutto was training colleagues in the same techniques of farming systems research developed earlier in Central America. Nationally, only a few senior agronomists had recognized the need for such location-specific research. Rutto was one of the first to embrace the idea and push it in the countryside. It was not just enhancement, in his view, but a matter of survival.

■

I found Rutto in the garden outside the district research station, not far from Kakamega center. "Yes," he said, "in some areas here population has drastically changed the situation from the days when corn hybrids first arrived." He stopped to look at some flowering beans, and smiled broadly. Rutto was a big man and as amiable as his shoulders were broad. He wore a dark sport coat and a white shirt with collar unbuttoned. "Before we began this round of on-farm research in the early '80s," he said, "we just *assumed* that three quarters of the farmers were still using the hybrid maize that came here in the '60s. But when we stopped to look at what farmers were *actually* doing, we found that—in some areas—the percentage was more like 20 percent, even when fertilizer and other inputs were available. I'm not denying that hybrids were widely used in the '60s and '70s—they were. Social and economic conditions simply changed the picture in some particular settings. We scientists were way behind that change. We were giving those farmers outdated advice based on conditions that existed twenty years before."

In the 1960s agronomists had recommended to highland farmers some hybrid seed varieties that produced taller plants.[9] The tall stalks gave higher yields per plant and allowed intercropping of vegetables in the space beneath the leaves. But the hybrids had a long seven-month maturation cycle, a characteristic destined to conflict with shrinking farm size. In the 1960s many farmers had still owned 20 acres. By the 1980s, as population grew and family landholdings were divided, the average farmer worked only a single acre. Farmers who stayed in Kakamega, especially on smaller plots, encountered a new difficulty with slow-maturing hybrids: They made possible only one crop per year. To compensate for reduced acreage, these farmers realized, they should try for two crops, not just one. Before long, they were switching wholesale from the slow-maturing hybrids to faster-maturing local varieties.

"You can see the irony," said Rutto. "In the '60s, as farmers adopted the hybrids, our research stations geared their own work to those varieties, thinking we were meeting local need. But you can't assume the old assumptions will always be right. We had to be ready

Jeremiah Rutto

to recognize that the social conditions in particular areas might be changing. Our research had to be area-specific and people-specific— understanding not just the environmental factors affecting crops in each area but the *social* and *economic* forces as well. We need to catch up with social change, or lose our scientific grip on the future of food."[10]

■

Debate over the ability of global agriculture to keep pace with population growth surfaced with particular force during the 1960s and early 1970s. The more pessimistic, echoing Malthusian fears, predicted a terrible era of "lifeboat ethics." The carrying capacity of earth and the productive capability of humans would simply be outstripped by exponential increases in birth rates. In the metaphor, people of rich countries occupied lifeboats at sea, the poor majority of the world swimming around them trying to get in. An awful dilemma confronted those in the boats: Should they honor their humanitarian obligation and save those who were drowning at the risk of overloading the boats?[11]

The fact that such fears had not been realized by the last decade of the twentieth century had much to do with successes in agricultural science in the '50s, '60s, and '70s. A nation like India, falling periodically into the clutches of famine—the classic "basket case"— reversed its vulnerability and became a food exporter within only a single generation. Though the country had certainly not solved its problems of food distribution, it had left behind the specter of sudden famine. India's reversal came largely through the development of a cadre of highly trained agricultural scientists and a network of research stations, and through policy changes more favorable to agriculture. International assistance in the training of Indian agronomists also played no small role. Importantly, the Indian research system took seriously the need to adapt crop research to local needs.[12] Later criticisms over the skewing of benefits toward better-off farmers, though often justified, do not negate the fact that small farmers also were great beneficiaries in many areas.[13] Following in India's wake were similar food successes in Indonesia and Pakistan. As one Pakistani economist put it, "Pakistan, India, Sri Lanka, even Bangladesh are better off than anyone ever would have expected a generation ago. Here are seven or eight countries with a billion people that had about five percent growth through the '80s. Add to that China—with a seven percent growth rate when they were opening up their economy—and you've got two billion out of the three billion in the Third World that have done remarkably well."[14]

In Kenya, however, the outcome of the race between population growth and food supply would not be known for several decades. Much would depend on whether family planning efforts succeeded in slowing the rate of new births. Some signs of progress were already evident by the late 1980s.[15] But even with a substantial decline in births, adequate food production would require progress in location-specific national research, and fast. The rapid advances in Asia suggested reasons for hope, given the right national and international support. But Kenya, like many African countries, faced shrinking national revenues. The possibility seemed remote in 1989 for finding major new resources for national research, let alone for investing in new efforts to understand and counter the impact of social change on local farmer needs. Even if funds were found tomorrow, political forces seemed locked in against new support for small-scale farming, which was also resisted by wealthier black African farmers who, since independence, had taken over the commercial farms of European settlers. Europeans had seen large-scale farming as the superior "modern" way. Their African successors took a similar view, and were making their voices heard in Nairobi. Meanwhile the Ministry of Agriculture, like many in Africa, was spreading its resources very thin across a large and bloated farm bureaucracy. Funds for reform were scarce. And as if to kill all hopes of advancing location-specific research, a government move to reorganize the research system, begun back in 1983, had by 1989 still failed to install a new director.

Some of those I found most distressed at delays in attacking Kenya's farm challenge were the ag-economists who originally came from CIMMYT in Mexico to share their techniques for determining and meeting the needs of small farms. From 1976 through the mid-1980s they had set up training programs in various East African countries, working out of their home office in Nairobi. Michael Collinson was the first head of the CIMMYT team. When I tracked Collinson down in the fall of 1989, he was no longer in Kenya, but looking abroad for ways to keep Africa's location-specific research alive. He had found considerable support from the lead coordinating agency in the international research system—the Consultative Group for International Agricultural Research (CGIAR). His office, located at the World Bank, was modest by Washingtonian standards but an executive suite compared to the narrow cubicle he had occupied back in Nairobi where I first visited him some years before. His brown hair had acquired a few more streaks of gray, and his square wire-rimmed glasses, British accent, and low-keyed congeniality hadn't changed, but he was now clearly worried. "It seems unbelievably difficult for a country like Kenya to change its priorities in favor of location-specific research," he said, "even when you can demonstrate the strengths of the process. One of the best things we in the international community can do is support change in the educational system. If you get advances there, you've fostered a change in basic attitudes. That's hard to measure in the short run but it can lead to the broad national change a country needs. That's what we're trying to do."[16]

Collinson took some solace that one of Kenya's leading colleges—Edgerton College—had decided to give the training program once administered by CIMMYT. What would come of a decade of efforts to train agronomists in Kenya—Collinson wasn't at all sure. "I don't know if it can still go forward and make a real difference for small farmer agriculture," he said. "But I also don't think it can just die on the vine. A generation of Kenyan researchers has seen some clear benefits from aligning research with social realities." He paused to look out the window. "And who knows, new government decisions could be for the best. They finally appointed a director of agricultural research—a fellow named Jeremiah Rutto. Haven't you two met?"

1. Isak Dinesen, *Out of Africa* and *Shadows on the Grass* (New York: Vintage Books of Random House, 1985, first published in 1937 and 1960, respectively). Beryl Markham is known for her book of short stories about growing up in Kenya, *West with the Night* (San Francisco: North Point Press, 1983, first published in 1942).

2. John Gerhart, *The Diffusion of Hybrid Maize in Western Kenya* (Mexico City: CIMMYT, 1975), abridged, pp. 26–27.

3. Gerhart, op. cit., p. 9.

4. Interview, summer 1987, with agricultural economist Malcolm Hall, then based in Nairobi.

5. CIMMYT's farming systems research training for the agronomists of East Africa was based in Nairobi with permission of the Government of Kenya, and training was provided Kenyan agronomists at the request of Kenyan agricultural authorities. Training activities were also undertaken in four other countries of East Africa—Ethiopia, Zambia, Malawi, and Tanzania.

6. Dinesen, op. cit., p. 4.

7. Norton-Griffiths was developing his data from his office at Ecosystems, Ltd., on contract for the Lake Basin Development Authority of the Government of Kenya.

8. The Norton-Griffiths thesis may apply well to some areas, but not others. For example, it has been criticized by some development specialists studying the effects caused by the movement of large numbers of Kenyans from the fertile highlands to settle and farm more agriculturally difficult and ecologically fragile land. According to Dr. Richard Ford of Clark University, farming practices learned in high-potential areas are then often applied to lower-potential lands with poor soils and less water. The result can be terrible degradation of already endangered land. Thus, Ford argues, in these lower-potential agricultural areas increased population density *can* and *does* translate into land degradation unless agricultural practices are more appropriate to the existing conditions. See Charity Kabutha & Richard Ford, "NGOs, Participation,

and Effective Resource Management in Marginal Areas: A Case Study of Mbusyani Sublocation" (Kenya) (Nairobi: Ministry of Environment and Natural Resources), mimeo.; and Barbara P. Thomas-Slayter, "Implementing Effective Local Management of Natural Resources: How Much Can NGOs Accomplish?" (Worcester, MA: Clark University, 1990), mimeo.

9. Some of the new tall-stalked hybrids yielded 40 percent more than existing shorter-stalked varieties (Gerhart, op. cit., p. 5).

10. For an overview of the broader challenge of farming systems research in eastern and southern Africa, see Mike Collinson, "The Development of African Farming Systems: Some Personal Views," *Agricultural Administration and Extension* 29(1988):7–22. The importance of location-specific research in Africa has gained much attention from agricultural scientists in the late 20th century. In addition to changing social conditions that must be monitored, Africa's large and diverse landscape has many more ecological zones than south and east Asia, with an enormous variety of insects and other ecological factors. For these reasons, a centralized research plan can seldom serve well the diverse need of large areas. According to Dr. Thomas Odhiambo, director of the ICIPE (International Centre for Insect Physiology and Ecology) research station in Nairobi, research in African settings must be as location-specific as possible, and be conceived as an ongoing process that also takes changing human needs into account (Interview, March 1987).

11. Garrett Hardin, "Lifeboat Ethics: The Case against Helping the Poor," *Psychology Today,* September 1974.

12. Uma Lele & Arthur A. Goldsmith, "The Development of National Agricultural Research Capacity: India's Experience with the Rockefeller Foundation and Its Significance for Africa" (Washington, DC: The World Bank Development Research Department, 1987), mimeo., p. 17. Regarding African research needs, Nile Brady of the U.S. Agency for International Development has observed: "Africa is the continent that can now most clearly benefit from an increased ability to generate and apply improved agricultural technologies. The variety and magnitude of agricultural constraints in that region are probably the worst in the world and have contributed to a decline in per capita food production over the last 20 years. Farmers in many parts of Africa must produce crops under different and very difficult conditions that often include low and unpredictable rainfall, acidic and infertile soils, and unique and hard-to-control animal and plant pests. Many Asians feel that the most important long-term outcome of development assistance was the building of university systems, sometimes very similar to the American land-grant model, that gave them the capacity to carry out their own agricultural research, educate their own researchers and technicians, and become the guardians of their natural resource base. We are now beginning to mount a similar 20 to 25 year effort in Africa. Within this plan, African countries will develop the capacity to generate improved agricultural technologies that will help them feed growing populations while they conserve their natural resource base and educate their own teachers, researchers, and extensionists" ("Reevaluating Substance and Process Priorities in Development Assistance," in *Food, Hunger, and Agricultural Issues* [Morrilton, AR: Winrock International Institute for Agricultural Development, 1989], p. 107).

13. Per Pinstrup-Andersen & Peter B. R. Hazell, "The Impact of the Green Revolution and Prospects for the Future," in M. Price Gittinger et al., eds., *Food Policy: Integrating Supply, Distribution, and Consumption* (Baltimore & London: Johns Hopkins University Press, 1987), pp. 106–118. For another assessment of the Green Revolution era and beyond, see Edward C. Wolf's "Beyond the Green Revolution: New

Approaches for Third World Agriculture," Worldwatch Paper no. 73 (Washington, DC: The Worldwatch Institute, October, 1986).

14. In the late 1980s, Dr. Mahbub ul Haq—after long experience in strategic planning for the World Bank and as Minister of Planning for the Pakistani government—concluded that the Asian experience should confirm the value of investment by the world community in *long-term* agricultural and economic development. "Asia is a vindication of the commitment to economic development over a longer period, supported by governmental reforms and aid from the international community. For a long period Asia was written off as a basket case—overcrowded, sluggish, economically inefficient—while those who advocated foreign aid and the idea of development as a process requiring long-term investment got ignored. It takes 25 to 30 years before institutions take firm root, infrastructure gets established, growth impulses are absorbed in systems of administration, law and order. . . . Yet because Latin America has temporarily run into difficulties due to a liquidity squeeze, and Africa still has to go through the transition they haven't had time to go through, people say foreign assistance is outmoded. In such a climate, unfortunately, the Latin Americans and Africans have come in low on the ladder of foreign assistance. It would be a tragedy if the lack of support would prevent the necessary infrastructure from moving into place. Because of the aid cushion we got in Asia, we had time to make the necessary policy changes. In my country of Pakistan, our development budget in the late '70s was 75 percent dependent on foreign assistance; now, in the late '80s, it is only 20 percent dependent. We want to bring it down to 5 percent. This is eloquent testimony to the positive role foreign assistance can play. But it must be given on a long-term basis" (Interview, January 1987, Islamabad).

15. Jane Perlez, "Birth Control Making Inroads in Populous Kenya," *New York Times*, September 10, 1989, p. 14.

16. Supporting such educational change is—for an international network like the CGIAR—equally as challenging as trying to transfer technologies used in temperate climates to people in the tropics. The "CG" had a strong track record in linking international know-how with local research needs in poor nations. In biogenetic research the CG encouraged national and regional research centers to identify problems and then used its own worldwide contacts to find university researchers able to help. When it came to location-specific research, Michael Collinson hoped that colleges within Kenya could, with assistance from research stations in the CG system, take on the training role. In this way the role international centers once played in spreading such training could become locally institutionalized without requiring large investments from financially strapped governments.

3

Excursion to Environmental Extremity: The Uncommon Logic of Change in West Africa's Parched Sahel

OUAGADOUGOU, BURKINA FASO

The ancient green forests of Burkina Faso had long since disappeared. Cattle grazing, tree cutting, farming without fallow, drought—all had conspired to strip the earth of its vegetation and fertility and to coax the sands of the Sahara to creep farther and farther south. Much of the country was now baked brown moonscape. Hybrid seeds that transformed other landscapes would not work here. International research centers were searching for ways simply to reclaim the land. Scores of development groups were urging farmers to plant new trees. Genetic engineers were trying to "design" plants to hold water, need less water to grow, and produce their own fertilizer as they grew. Yet few experts held out much hope that results would come in time for this generation of Burkinabe to benefit—until a curiously simple device appeared, made of two notched sticks and a piece of thin plastic tube.

April 1985. They had come to Ouagadougou, the capital of Burkina Faso, from all over West Africa, and from North America. These were the elite of the agriculture community—agronomists, plant breeders, genetic engineers, farm college administrators, agricultural economists, anthropologists.[1] Burkina, as a country, embodied the dilemmas of their research. Located at the center of West Africa's Sahel, it had suffered some of the severest effects of drought in all of Africa. The worst years were 1983 and 1984, although the regularity of annual rains had been steadily tapering off since the 1960s—

ironically, a period when newly independent nations most needed sure rainfall.[2] At a conference center in Ouagadougou, scientist after scientist braved the afternoon heat and took the platform to outline new dimensions of the research agenda for sub-Saharan Africa. The audience began to nod off. Perhaps it was the heat, perhaps the realization that some key applications of research were still twenty years away, or perhaps the fact that so little could be done at all until better ways were devised to capture the little rain that did fall.

A young soil and water engineer took his turn at the platform. Peter Wright wanted to talk not about high-tech seeds but about water. Wright had first come to Burkina as a Peace Corps volunteer. After returning to the United States to study water management at the University of Arizona, he had returned to Burkina, learned the local Mori language, and began exploring the problems of water control in the northern part of the country, backed by the relief and development agency Oxfam UK. After years of experimentation and discussion with farmers, he now told the conference on drylands agriculture he had found a method that enabled farmers to capture and control water at a cost they could actually afford. The main components, Wright explained, were two sticks, a segment of clear plastic tubing, and the small rocks found all across the West African landscape.

Looking on from the back of the room was Dr. Peter Matlon, chief economist for the West African programs of ICRISAT, the International Crops Research Institute for Semi-Arid Tropics.[3] Matlon watched as drowsy listeners woke up across the room. Leaving the conference later that day, Matlon registered his amazement to friends: "It's astonishing how a presentation about this simple device can electrify senior colleagues. You see how the logic of change here in the Sahel keys so powerfully to water and environment. There's no question we're going to have breakthroughs in the high-tech areas—they're happening. But those will only go so far unless we do better at capturing rain, and in ways poor farmers can afford. Assumptions about seed research also get turned around here. We're only beginning to crack the logic of reversing the desert."[4]

■

Even before my plane landed at Ouagadougou, the desert left no doubt we were entering its domain. On the approach to Ouagadougou from the south, the sight of cloudless skies from the window seemed to augur a landing in perfect view of the broad West African flatlands. But as the plane descended, visibility suddenly vanished. A reddish-brown smoke seemed to have swallowed the aircraft. Talk in the cabin dropped to a hush; half-formed questions rose in a whisper: Engine on fire? War zone? As fast as sight left, it returned, almost like breaking through a low-lying cloud to a hazy atmosphere below. On the ground the taxi driver explained, "Oh, we're used to this. In the dry months of March and April sands from the Sahara get caught up into the sky by rising drafts of wind. These dust clouds respect neither man nor beast below. A fine white dust also rains from the sky. We have a name for it." With his finger he wrote a word in the dust on the front seat: HARMATTAN.

In the years since Burkina gained independence in 1960, the people (Burkinabe) had been adapting to longer and longer periods of Harmattan. Rains that once returned regularly from May to October were becoming scarce and erratic, drying up what little hope remained for the nation's economy, routinely ranked by the World Bank among the poorest in the world. But if such troubles could be explained, in part, by environmental forces beyond human control, by the late 1980s the Burkinabe were less willing to accept a future of unmitigated hardship. Modern communications were raining still another dust over the popular mind, an information dust that raised new hopes for the "good life" experienced in neighboring countries and abroad. Rural Burkinabe were also being exposed to enticing life-styles in the capital city of Ouagadougou (pronounced wa-ga-doo-goo), increasing their appetites for better-quality food. This "aspiration explosion," especially among the younger generations, played no small part in the four military coups of the 1980s.[5]

After the '83 and '87 coups, desperation about the future fueled radical swings of national politics. The '83 coup brought to power Thomas Sankara, an army captain in his mid-30s. Sankara introduced one of the most austere brands of socialism West Africa had ever seen. He called for national self-reliance and encouraged Burkinabe to buy only locally produced foods and products. He cut back on the salaries and jobs of civil servants, bringing the rural people to center stage in national development. While rechanneling some investment from urban to rural development, he also promoted voluntarism and self-help in the countryside, sometimes with forced mobilizations for public projects. And he introduced a rhetoric of national pride, changing the country's name from Upper Volta to Burkina Faso, "Land of the Upright People."[6] Four short years later, many in government and in the countryside felt exhausted by the severity of reform and the lack of visible results. In October 1987 Sankara was assassinated at the initiative of one of his closest friends and confidants, Captain Blaise Compaore, and the country once more plunged into change. This time market forces and capitalism were given freer play. And while the new government continued to call for national self-reliance, one of its first acts reopened the doors to the outside world, easing restrictions on fruits and vegetables from abroad.[7]

But the question remained: What could be done about agriculture at home? Seventy percent of the country's income came from agriculture, and 80 percent of Burkinabe earned their living from it.[8] Since 1970, Burkina and the other nations of sub-Saharan Africa had comprised the only region in the world where population growth rates were outpacing food production. In the Sahel, the nations bordering the southern rim of the Sahara desert, population would double in 25 years.[9] Unless agriculture could make significant advances, African analysts held out little hope that Sahelians would ever better their standards of living.[10] That meant meeting some of the toughest challenges of water control and seed development in the world—which is why I sought to learn more from ICRISAT's Peter Matlon.

Matlon agreed to meet me at the Hotel Independence in Ouagadougou (Wa-ga, as locals call it). I found him sitting under a large umbrella near the outdoor pool, one of the very few oases in town. The afternoon heat, which persuades almost everyone just to rest indoors, was beginning to break. Matlon was a slender, soft-spoken, but eloquent man with dark thinning hair and a look not unlike pop singer Paul Simon. "Much of the farm research here got unduly influenced by excitement over the Green Revolution in Asia and Central America," he said. "The idea behind that revolution was so seductive that African researchers jumped uncritically on the bandwagon, with some disappointing results. In effect, Green Revolution methods changed the environment to fit high-yielding seeds. In other words, you had seeds that were highly responsive to water and fertilizer, you then increased the levels of water and nutrients in the environment, and you got a little energy-converting factory that was highly efficient. But here in the Sahel, we don't have sure means for enhancing the environment. Rainfall is too erratic. The Sahelian governments are too poor and inefficient to ensure that farmers will get the fertilizer they need. So rather than starting with high-yield seeds, we have to start with realities of the environment that so directly affect farmers. Once we understand the problems posed by the realities, then we seek out seeds and techniques that will serve farmers best. You see how the logic differs from the Green Revolution in its classic form?"[11]

The "realities" facing the farmers of Burkina included shallow soils with nutrients severely depleted over the years, acidity reaching crop-threatening levels, and, because of poor structure, an inability to retain water. When rain did arrive in "normal" years, most of it washed away, carrying with it still more of the little topsoil that remained. Matlon leaned out from the umbrella's shade, looked up at the white sun that peered through Harmattan haze, and mopped his brow. "Even the high-performing seeds developed by ICRISAT in India have not done well here. We brought over some of those seeds, but found that under the stresses of soil and climate they get very irregular results. Our soils and water control don't compare with India's, even in the semi-arid zones there."[12]

Contrary to assumptions that stand up well in other parts of the world, ICRISAT researchers had to abandon their search in the 1970s and early 1980s for high-yielding seeds, highly responsive to water and fertilizer. Instead they looked for seeds a notch lower on the scale, that would respond to extra water and fertilizer when they were available but also survive without them. By the late 1980s, seed breeders had, in fact, identified some promising varieties of millet and sorghum fitting that description. More than 3,000 types of millet and 7,000 types of sorghum were screened before the right ones were found.[13] Meanwhile, the search for new means of water control followed a similar pattern of stepping back in order to go ahead. Since the farmers of Burkina could not afford irrigation, researchers looked for methods sufficiently simple and cheap to be of practical use. "The two-stick method is the most hopeful thing we've seen in decades," said Matlon. "If you get basic water control, you can begin to do other things to reclaim the desert. It's quite a sight where that method gets used. You'll be driving across an utterly barren brown landscape, and suddenly you come to a hillside covered by a strip of green. That, in desert terms, means you're doing something right."

■

Driving north out of Burkina's capital the next day, I stopped at a cafe in an isolated outpost near Ouahigouya hoping to pick up a development worker named Mathieu Ouedraogo. If the lonely pony express offices in America's wild West could be said to have an African counterpart, this site in northern Burkina would certainly be it. Clustered along the Harmattan-swept highway were a general store, a pub, and a post office, the barren flatlands stretching in all directions as far as the eye could see. Mathieu Ouedraogo was waiting in the pub. Over the years he had become expert in training local farmers in land-regenerating techniques. As the French put it: an *animateur par exellence*—superb mover and teacher. Ouedraogo was a different cut from Kenya's Jeremiah Rutto. Rutto was an educated outsider who went to remote villages to bring new knowledge "in." Ouedraogo was an insider, the son of a family in the area he served, working year after year in the extended neighborhood he had known from youth. While he had not attended college, he spoke fluent French and had proved his effectiveness in helping villagers grasp the potential and costs of new methods. In some ways his "uneducated effectiveness" impressed private development agencies more than the abilities of "experts" trained outside. As one Oxfam worker put it, "Here you have a fellow who begins his career with water control experiments in the late '70s, and is still building on those early efforts a decade later. He's got an excellent knowledge of the area and of the new water technologies. In his teaching he uses local Mossi proverbs to bring out the advantages of new techniques. This more than compensates for the lack of formal training. And people who *do* get outside training often refuse to come back and share what they've learned. The training never bears local fruit."[14]

Mathieu Ouedraogo emerged from the pub and suggested we take his truck the rest of the journey. The road to Ouahigouya traversed baked, parched countryside, cutting in and out of the eroded ravines that had channeled Burkina's runoff water for generations. Caught in small whirlwinds along the roadside, sand columns danced like desert dervishes. Across the landscape, trees occasionally dared to break through the cracked earth. Most were now leafless skeletons, giving the landscape a ghostly quality not unlike the aftermath of a forest fire. The occasional full-branched tree almost invariably attracted to the ground below it a cluster of thatch-roofed family huts, jealously guarding their place in the shade. "I know older people," said Mathieu Ouedraogo, "who remember their youth when the forest was thick all around, with more wild animals than you could count. The soils were abundant and deep; now we dig and reach bedrock only a few inches down." Along the roadside were remnants of small check dams built to control water runoff. Most had silted up and caved in—the legacy of hundreds of hasty, ill-advised efforts by the government and by private relief groups to do something about water.[15]

Ouedraogo signaled a turnoff to a farm where the two-stick method was being used. "Strangely enough," he said, "we have no shortage of land out here, but everybody is concentrating into small areas, incredibly overcrowded. This happens because water rushes off the land, carrying with it the topsoil. The soil then deposits in lowland areas. Of course, everyone wants to live near good soil. So they abandon vast stretches of land that were once quite productive. Our new water control methods contour the land with small rock dams, blocking the flow of water. We call them *diguettes*. They make it possible to reclaim much of the land farmers like these were once tempted to abandon."

About fifty yards out from the local farmers' family huts, Ouedraogo pointed to long lines of rocks piled six to ten inches high. As we approached, I began to see how the diguettes formed curving lines across the landscape, something like the lines of a contour map. One curve was followed by another some fifteen to twenty feet away, then another, and another, forming concentric rings that hinted at an imaginary center in the distance.

"What you cannot see with the naked eye is that this land actually slopes up gradually to points that are higher and higher out there in the distance. Though we cannot perceive the slope, you can be sure the water does. From the highest points it was just rushing off. Now each line of rock dikes holds water up to a certain level, and the overflow gets captured in the next lower contour. For the first time farmers have been able to hold water long enough to get crops and

trees planted. The crop increases have been spectacular—sometimes over a ton per hectare."[16]

The sun began to drop lower in the hazy Harmattan sky, producing a white glow more like moonset than the warm pink sunsets I had come to know in other Sahelian countries. The head of the household, an elderly Burkinan named Sunimal Alles, approached with two of his sons. Farmer Alles was wearing sandals, orange pants, and a long-draping burgundy robe whose V-neck top was decorated with gold embroidery. He held upright two wooden rods, about five feet tall, whose tops were connected to the open ends of a clear plastic tube that hung to the ground in the shape of a "U." Water inside the tube rose on both sides to areas of notch marks carved on the wooden poles. Here, then, was the long-awaited secret to contouring land and holding precious rain.

"This is how it works," explained farmer Alles in the Mori tongue. "The water will always rise to the same height in each end of the tube. That is the character of water. When one stick is standing on higher ground than the other, the level of the water comes to different notch levels on the sticks. To find where two points of ground are level, we just move one stick until the water level on both sticks comes to the same notch. Then we mark where the sticks are, and link up these points with diguettes. Simple!" Mathieu Ouedraogo laughed, grasping farmer Alles around the shoulder. "It's not really that simple," Ouedraogo explained, "when you realize it took Peter Wright years of discussions with farmers and years of field experimentation to get this method in an affordable form that farmers could master in a few days' training."[17]

By the late 1980s hundreds of farms in the north of Burkina had been treated with diguettes, representing over 2,000 hectares of land. The World Bank was putting additional "muscle" behind getting the good news out to farmers who had not yet heard, multiplying the outreach efforts many times over.[18] As word of the diguette technique spread, farmers from all over northern Burkina and from neighboring Mali and Niger were also visiting Mathieu Ouedraogo's demonstration fields. Meanwhile, newly achieved water control triggered other plans to enhance farming systems. "Farmers themselves immediately see the possibilities," said Mathieu Ouedraogo, "and their orders of priority have not always been ours. Back in the '70s we began urging them to plant trees so that the land could recover forest and the soils be held down by the roots. But farmers themselves wanted first to plant more crops. Food security came first. Once that was there, they did plant trees, forming natural fences to keep cattle from wandering and making it possible to gather manure for better crop fertilization. Whole farm systems are now getting much more efficient. All this has called even my own worst fears into question. When I was a kid I had nightmares that the desert would devour us forever. I thought we would never get back the lands we had lost. Now I am not so sure."[19]

1. The conference, which took place April 2–5, 1985, was staged by Purdue University in cooperation with research centers in western Africa and the U.S. Agency for International Development (AID).

2. On the pattern of diminishing rainfall in sub-Saharan Africa after 1960, see charts in P. Lamb, cited in Michael H. Glantz, ed., *Drought and Hunger in Africa: Denying Famine a Future* (Cambridge: Cambridge University Press, 1987), p. 39; and Thomas S. Jayne, John C. Day, & Harold E. Dregne, "Technology and Agricultural Productivity in the Sahel" (Washington, DC: U.S. Department of Agriculture, Economic Research Service, October 1989), p. 5.

3. ICRISAT, part of the international network of research centers around the world, has headquarters in Hyderabad, India. The main West African branch is located in Niamey, Niger.

4. For an overview of applications of genetic engineering research, see Charles S. Gasser & Robert T. Fraley, "Genetically Engineering Plants for Crop Improvement," *Science*, June 16, 1989, 244: 1293–99. One particularly hopeful development came in the late 1980s when American researchers isolated a gene in pearl millet that raises yields under drought conditions by nearly 25 percent (Dennis Avery, "News from the Center for Global Food Issues" [Indianapolis: Hudson Institute, November 1989], p. 4).

5. Explained Dr. John Becker, an agricultural specialist working for the U.S. Agency for International Development: "This country's economic problems get too easily blamed on the drought or aid. But such explanations, in my view, mask the more fundamental problem of people's rapidly rising expectations, which are hard to fulfill" (Interview, March 1985).

6. The sense of anger and despair was typified in an address by Sankara before the United Nations in 1984. Clad in dress fatigues and red beret, he vented his frustration about the state of poverty in Burkina, as well as about aid from the West. "Very few countries have been inundated with as much aid as mine, but look at the wretchedness we inherited." Sankara lamented that out of Burkina's 7 million people, 6 million remain impoverished peasants, infant mortality is 180 per thousand, and average per capita income is only $100. Development specialists, he said, were sending the developing countries back to the world of slavery. (Reported in *The New York Times*, October 5, 1984).

7. *The Economist* Intelligence Unit (EIU) Country Profile 1988–89, pp. 29 and 32, and EIU Country Profile, No. 4, 1988, Togo, Niger, Benin, Burkina, pp. 8 and 30. As the EIU described the five-year development plan for 1986–90, "Like its predecessor, the 1986–90 plan places strong emphasis on attaining national economic independence and mobilising the populace in support of development schemes. Among its objectives are major investments in the agricultural sector (almost 20 per cent of planned spending), the development of water resources (24 per cent), the continuation of the fight against desertification, an improvement in the quality of life, particularly for women, who account for a substantial part of the work force, a greater degree of integration between the different sectors of the economy and a reduction in regional disparities" (EIU Country Profile 1988–89, pp. 32–33).

8. In all the Sahelian countries, 80 percent of the 38 million people are supported by rainfed agriculture. And this despite the fact that less than 4 percent of the land is fit for cultivation (Jayne et al., op. cit., p. 6).

9. Jayne et al., op. cit., p. 4.

10. As Michael F. Lofchie put it, "Since world demand for [export] commodities is projected to grow only slowly at best between now and the end of this century, Africa's prospects of developing an adequate foreign exchange earning capacity must necessarily lie in the introduction of agricultural policies that will enable the continent to recapture its former share of world trade in these commodities. This would require a major and politically difficult diversion of national resources away from urban industries and services to the countryside. . . . Unless there is a major reversal of current trends in the agricultural sector, there is little basis for optimism about Africa's economic future" (Glantz, op. cit., pp. 88–89). According to Delgado, Mellor, and Blackie, the centrality of the food and nonfood agricultural sector in sub-Saharan Africa has to do with the fact that domestic food production occupies such a high proportion of the labor force, that improved productivity could provide major increases in national income, that improving food production is less subject than export commodities to external price uncertainties, and that trade of foodstuffs in the region is likely to increase greatly through the end of the century (John W. Mellor, Christopher L. Delgado, & Malcolm J. Blackie, *Accelerating Food Production in Sub-Saharan Africa* [Baltimore: Johns Hopkins University Press, 1987], pp. 4–5).

11. Elsewhere Matlon observed that initially encouraging good results in on-station experiments with improved varieties of sorghum and millet have frequently been followed in West Africa by 40 to 60 percent yield gaps when improved seeds are actually tried on farms, resulting in high risks of financial loss and low adoption rates among farmers. Improved varieties from India and elsewhere, he added, often run into difficulties because of the inadequacies of West African soils (discussed below), weak infrastructure and thus inefficient delivery systems, and susceptibility to local diseases. In addition, the new varieties are often found by locals to have undesirable taste and storage characteristics (Mellor et al., op. cit., pp. 71–72 and 76).

12. In an interview with the author, Peter Matlon observed that "The soils are substantially better in the semi-arid tropics of Asia than they are here. You've got large pockets of high-potential alluvial soils and vertisols—the deep black soils, high in clay content, high in organic matter, which have good water-holding capacity and which have adequate levels of soil nutrients. What success we've had in India with sorghum hybrid varieties has been in these vertisol areas, or in irrigated areas. The presence of vertisols in West Africa is insignificant—probably well under two to three percent of the cultivatable areas. What predominates here is soils with low clay content, low natural fertility, and acidification caused by intensive continuous cropping with few periods of letting the land lie fallow. In addition, the soils are very shallow, structurally less porous, tend to harden during the dry season, resulting in serious water runoff when the rains arrive" (Interview, April 1985). For more details on the problems of soil in western Africa, see Mellor et al., op. cit., pp. 60–62, and R. Nicou & C. Charreau, "Soil Tillage and Water Conservation in Semi-Arid West Africa," in *Appropriate Technologies for Farmers in Semi-Arid West Africa* (West Lafayette, IN: Purdue University Press, 1985), pp. 9–32.

13. As Jayne, Day, & Dregne put it, "New seed varieties should be capable of outperforming traditional varieties at low levels of management and fertilization, reflecting the current low-input orientation in the Sahel. . . . The poor record of [high-yielding varieties] adopted in the region has been traced to excessive emphasis on input-dependent varieties that provide high yields under controlled research-station

conditions, which bear little resemblance to typical subsistence farm conditions. The dramatic [high-inputs]-driven yield increases of the Green Revolution in Asia may not be expected in the Sahel unless agronomic and input-marketing constraints are alleviated" (op. cit., p. 20).

14. Interview, April 1989, with Peter Wright.

15. They either lacked the technical qualities to hold up over time or had the engineering precision in construction but villagers were not suitably trained to keep them from eventually silting up. In the 1960s a large program was mounted by the European Development Fund to use bulldozers to build low earth dikes along the contours of the land. Unfortunately, local people were not involved in the planning and did not keep up the earthen dikes, and animals broke through, allowing the water to escape (Paul Harrison, "Fragile Future," supplement in the *Observer*, May 4, 1988, p. 12). Christopher Reij ("The Present State of Soil and Water Conservation in the Sahel" [Amsterdam: Free University's Working Group for Resource Development in Africa, September 1988], paper submitted to the Club du Sahel) confirms that on lands treated in the '60s, '70s, and early '80s with earth "bunding," the bunding was generally not maintained by the farmers, and only their traces can now be found (op. cit., p. 3, para. 11). The EIU Country Profile 1988–89 points out that "The CNR government [Captain Thomas Sankara's Conseil National de la Révolution] gave a very high priority to the construction of earth dams, to conserve water, and the digging of wells for irrigation. These programmes had some success, despite suffering technical shortcomings in many cases," but adds, "Construction of small earth dams was another project dear to Captain Sankara's heart, on the basis that it demonstrated what could be achieved at the local level with voluntary labour. However, a number of the dams were hastily built and collapsed when they began to fill" (op. cit., pp. 35 and 41). One gets an idea of the multitude of development agencies working in the late 1980s on soil and water problems in north central Burkina from the list compiled by Christopher Reij (named by acronym): ADRK, AFVP, CECI, HIMO (ILO), LVIA, Oxfam, PDZT, PPI, PAE, CDRY, Six S, PEDI (Dutch bilateral aid), Projet Petits Barrages (Caritas Burkinabe), Projet d'Aménagement des terroirs (GTZ), FEER (World Bank/Dutch bilateral aid), and IFAD (op. cit., p. 22).

16. This observation may be modest for some areas. Reij cites studies in 1986 showing that yields on 33 fields treated with stone bunds averaged 972 kg/ha, whereas yields on 33 untreated fields averaged 612 kg/ha (op. cit., p. 8, para. 22).

17. Experimentation with various types of contouring had actually been going on in Burkina for many decades. Some of the first were begun at the turn of the century by Mossi tribesmen trying to deal with runoff on steeper slopes (Reij, op. cit., p. 16, para. 40). In the 1960s French engineers tried other experiments, but farmers rejected them as too costly or simply unsustainable over time. The farmers rapidly embraced the rock ridging technique, knowing they could find rocks in abundance across the countryside, had the surplus labor needed for building the contour ridges, and, most importantly, could afford the time and labor to do it (Reij, op. cit., p. 7, para. 11).

18. The so-called Training and Visitation System of the World Bank, originated by Daniel Ben Orr, an agricultural extension specialist with the World Bank.

19. Reij argued that much greater investment would be necessary if land reclamation were to be significant. "If the present rate of construction of conservation works was to be maintained, it would take several centuries . . . before the cultivated area now needing conservation measures will be treated. This leads to the conclusion that unless the present rate of implementation of conservation works can be increased ten times or more, there is little chance of reversing the continuing degradation of the cultivated area" (op. cit.).

PART TWO

Power and the Powerless

4

Playing Forces at the Top for Advantage at the Bottom

ISLAMABAD, PAKISTAN

When Jamil Nishtar first became head of the Agricultural Develop-
ment Bank of Pakistan in 1978, rural poverty was on the rise. Small
farmer incomes in much of the country were not keeping pace with
those in more favored agricultural zones. More and more rural
people—still 70 percent of the population—were migrating to swol-
len cities. To help reverse the rural decline, Nishtar set out to reform
the entire system of rural banking, opening new services for small
farmers in nearly all of Pakistan's 35,000 villages. He did it through
a system of "bankers on bikes"—young agronomists who traversed
the countryside on motorcycles, taking the bank where people actu-
ally live. But Nishtar's accomplishments for people at the grass-
roots followed quieter, but perhaps even more significant, moves at
higher levels of power.

Harvard economist Dick Goldman reached for his cup of tea and
took a sip. "So what was it, then, about Nishtar that made him
stand apart? Now that some months have passed since he died, we
should be able to see things more clearly." For a moment my attention shifted from a sidewalk cafe in Harvard Square in the summer
of 1989 to my first interview with A. Jamil Nishtar in an office in
Islamabad six years before. I could still see him standing by his
executive office window, as if it were happening all over. Nishtar's
persona tended to imprint itself indelibly on the mind. He was

wearing traditional Pakistani garb—baggy light-brown *shalwar* trousers and long-sleeve, collarless *kurta* shirt of the same color, cut to hang like a smock from shoulder to knee; over the shirt, his vestlike *sherwani*, a dark-brown sleeveless coat that fell from shoulder to hip, was left unbuttoned down the front. If the garb was traditional, it was instantly apparent that this was no back-to-simplicity traditionalist. Nishtar had risen through Pakistan's most sophisticated financial ranks to become one of its senior bankers. He projected an air of cool authority, reinforced by a tall, full-bodied physique. His black hair, graying at the temples, was perfectly parted on the side. His broad puffy face sported horn-rimmed glasses, a bushy white mustache brushed out to the sides, and his trademark—a smoke-effusing pipe that seldom left the corner of his mouth. Why, I wondered back then, had a senior banker of his rank wanted to take on the reform of a listless, floundering bank for rural development?

My attention returned to the sidewalk cafe in Massachusetts, and Goldman's question. "When you ask what made Nishtar stand apart, Dick, I think of two things. The first is what people always talk about—the way he transformed a national bank so that it could work for poorer rural people who normally got no benefit. But none of that would have happened in the '70s and '80s without the other thing he did. Nishtar, it seems to me, had the ability to play forces at the top. This you never hear about. Somehow he got the forces of national and international power behind what he was doing for people at the grassroots. There was an extraordinary pragmatism about the way he operated." Goldman paused to reflect. Over the years he had observed economic planners in a variety of developing country settings. "Yes," he said, "there are a lot of visionary people in these leadership positions who fail to have much lasting impact. If they have vision and political charisma, they often don't have the managerial skill to translate that vision into a working reality. Or they're effective managers but can't generate a politically attractive vision. To do what happened in Pakistan, Nishtar must have had both—the managerial skill and vision to get the political preconditions right. You watched him—what did he do to pull it off?"

"Well, images come to mind. There was a flight from New Delhi to Islamabad. I was scheduled to meet with Nishtar for the second time."

∎

The flight to Islamabad in the spring of 1987 roused dormant memories of the tense and fragile ambiguity that is Pakistan. I had flown the same route in 1984—southwest from Delhi to Pakistan's seaport of Karachi, then up to the capital, Islamabad, in a mountain valley of the north. Now, as the Pakistani airliner made its way from Karachi northward along the fabled Indus River, I compared notes from my previous trip with news of more recent events. The political ambiguities had not disappeared: on one hand, the disciplined civil order of a country under military rule; on the other, the lurking forces of disruption and rebellion, the fear that things might fall apart, that the center won't hold. As if to keep the forces of order always in view, official press headlines continued to publicize the workings of Pakistan's corps of professional civil servants and economic planners; the campaigns to "Islamicize" all aspects of public life; the tranquility of relations with other countries; the absence of war with India; amicable relations with powers like China, Japan, the United States, and moderate Arab states of the Middle East.

But every headline proclaiming civility and order seemed to have chillier, more unsettling undercurrents. The persistence of military rule was itself a symbol of underlying civil unrest. General-cum-President Zia ul-Haq continued to renege on promises to hold national elections. Political rallies led by opposition leader Benazir Bhutto would not let the nation forget the coup that brought General Zia to power ten years before and led to the execution of her father, Prime Minister Zulfikar Ali Bhutto. National unity also strained under the pulls of regional factionalism—Pathans to the northwest, Baluchis to the southwest, Punjabis to the northeast, Sindhis to the southeast, and three million ferociously independent Afghan refugees who had crossed the northwest frontier to escape Soviet tanks. Meanwhile, sharp reminders of the fragility of international peace still surfaced—military standoffs with Indian forces at the eastern border, bitter accusations from America that Pakistan was secretly building nuclear weapons, the intrusions of Soviet-made Afghan jets into Pakistani airspace, the strafing of camps suspected of harboring anti-Soviet guerrillas.

No planner of rural reform, Jamil Nishtar included, could attempt such reform in isolation from the tense ambiguities that played upon Pakistan's political subconscious. Conversely, reforms in the countryside were bound to affect those ambiguities, pressing toward either stability or dissolution. Countries like South Korea and Taiwan had invested heavily in their rural economies, which had paid off handsomely, not only improving the lot of farmers but also promoting industrial growth and national security. In Iran, by contrast, the Shah had failed to take rural needs seriously, a failure that sowed the seeds of revolution and the downfall of one of the brashest imperial rulers of modern times.[1]

As the plane touched down at Islamabad's airport, I was hoping to go immediately into the countryside to see how the "bankers on bikes" were doing, then to corner Nishtar and his colleagues later at bank headquarters. But that was not to be. I was met by a driver who suggested I "might first want to see the Chairman." This, I knew, meant Nishtar first wanted to see *me*. He always seemed to be a step ahead of business, never behind. Driving into view of the building Nishtar had constructed to house the Agricultural Development Bank of Pakistan (ADBP), I felt once again the aura of modernity he tried to project. It was a high-rise office block reminiscent of I. M. Pei's more monumental concrete structures. Two white concave towers, joined back to back, rose gleaming in the sun, far above the sprawl of government buildings. "Tallest building in Islamabad," said my guide, as if to say Pakistan is now giving agriculture a priority it never had before.

This time the man in the Chairman's top-floor office was wearing not traditional Pakistani garb but the pinstripes of a Western banker. His distinctive features hadn't changed—the black hair graying at the temples, the horn-rimmed glasses, the bushy white mustache, the trademark pipe. "Good to see you again," he said. "You must see more of what's going on in the countryside. We're now reaching the farthest corners. And the whole thing is computerized. Before you go out to the field, you should tour the computer system here at headquarters. But first, we can talk." I thanked him and we sat down. "I've been meaning to ask you, Mr. Chairman, why did you get involved in this effort in the first place? Why the shift from urban banking to a rural enterprise like this?"

Nishtar lit a match and put the flame to his pipe tobacco. "Really, it's very simple," he said. "I long suspected that rural banking—done right—could trigger great benefits for Pakistan. You must remember that in most underdeveloped countries, including our own, a modern banking system was inherited from colonial rulers—in our case,

John Schnell

the British. But this system had actually been holding us back for decades. The British were not really interested in developing our country; they wanted to export cotton to their textile mills in Lancashire. So the banking system they designed served urban traders and cotton plantations. It was totally inappropriate for agriculture, especially the small farmers who comprise three quarters of our people. Even by the 1970s we had not really figured out how to do agricultural lending. An agricultural development bank had been operating for decades, but the default rate was running over 50 percent. Something had to change. I wanted to see if the old banking model—designed for urban traders—could be transformed into one that would work for agriculture."

Nishtar spoke with the eloquence one might expect of a Cambridge-trained economist. His English combined a British

49

lilt—acquired during his graduate student days in England—and a variation of the South Asian English that evolved within elite Pakistani circles since independence in the late 1940s. Elite schooling and a career in the country's upper economic echelons were perhaps inevitable for one whose father had been a founder of post-British Pakistan. But Nishtar's speech also betrayed the commoner in him—a round-voweled accent and slightly florid expressions that derived from Urdu, the language he had learned while growing up among Pathan people near the northwest frontier. Though educationally and bureaucratically at the top, Nishtar wanted to make it clear he had not lost touch with the less advantaged.

"It took decades," he went on, "for intellectuals to realize that real development means *people*, not things. In the '50s and '60s our banks and the international banks were investing in *things*—buildings, roads, airports, factories. These things were important for our economy. But by the 1970s we realized that growth still wasn't benefiting the majority of people. We needed to stop investing in things and invest in *people*, especially those in the countryside.[2] This also meant that banking could no longer be seen as the mere lending of money; loans would have to be coupled with information and services so that disadvantaged people could reach for new productivity. In short, we began to conceive credit as an instrument of *development*. This is what we've done through our Mobile Credit Officers, the MCOs."

He took several puffs, then took the pipe from his lips. "Quite remarkable what these MCOs are doing—I want you to go out farther into the countryside this time. Then come back and we'll talk some more."

■

Traveling by motorcycle across the rocky dirt roads of Pakistan's northwest frontier, one quickly learns that there is a price to pay for "taking the bank to the poor." It is partly a matter of logistics: physical distances to be overcome, gaping vast spaces separating remote village communities from the centers of commerce. To close the gap requires investment not only of money but of human time and energy. I had first taken Nishtar's comments about "investing in people" with a grain of skepticism—too many rural development schemes launched with grand rhetoric have failed to materialize in services rendered. But within barely an hour of riding shotgun on the motorbike of an MCO, I was convinced of Nishtar's determination to make his bank real to the remote and disadvantaged, whatever the cost.

Kifayat Ali, an MCO in the northwest frontier region, had agreed to show me the route to his farthest clients and what it takes to actually reach them. After we turned off the main highway leading out of Peshawar, the roads became unpaved, hilly, and liberally sprinkled with holes. Speed is not easily achieved under such conditions, although the motorbike is far superior to the animal cart or bicycle. That simple fact buoys Kifayat Ali during the twenty-one days he must be on the road each month. Like all MCOs, he had been assigned to serve in the region where he grew up. He was a graduate of one of the region's agricultural colleges.[3] It was now his job to visit borrowers in twenty-five villages at least once a month, handing out loans, resolving problems, and doing everything possible to ensure that clients get the know-how and inputs they need to make profits. Without this, a bank could never expect its loans to be repaid. To reach the remoter farmers, Ali was prepared to take rodeolike punishment, at times more than a hundred kilometers of it. "There are rewards," he assured me, shouting above the noise of his galloping Honda engine. "As a Mobile Credit Officer, you are actually given the bike; you own it. The bank also pays us well. And I grew up here. There's a satisfaction in doing something for these people. They've had little opportunity before."

I knew that another of Ali's motives may have gone unspoken. It had to do with a narrow, and troubled, stretch of land about two hours to the west. There the Hindu Kush mountains divide Pakistan from neighboring Afghanistan. And there, at the Khyber Pass, multitudes of Afghan refugees had poured across the border since the late 1970s, enormously straining the region's economy. I had visited the Pass days before. On the surface it is a desolate forty-mile stretch of highway cutting through a mountainous moonscape of greenish-brown gravel. But for anyone aware of its history, one gaze at the Pass is enough to stir the blood. Every major invasion of India had come through the Pass, from Alexander the Great in the fourth century B.C. to the Moghuls in the sixteenth. The image of a dashing young Alexander, commanding chariot fleets and endless ranks of foot soldiers, is still enshrined in local folklore and art. The ancient hills still seem to echo with ghostly shouts of invading hordes from Central Asia. But the invaders of the 1980s were refugees—three million Afghans fleeing from Soviet tanks and helicopter gunships, all in need of food and shelter. The majority had settled in camps set up by the United Nations. Others had built mud houses in the mountain valleys, trying to maintain their independence, and their guns. Nishtar, a native of the northwest frontier, liked to taunt the Russian invaders across the border: "They don't realize it," he said, "but their presence has given our tribesmen a vocation. It's brought some real fun into their lives—daily target practice."

Under such surface gibes, however, lurked deeper fears, fears of economic overload in the region, fears that refugees would stake claim to the land and never leave. In the worst nightmare, Russian troops would someday enter the Pass trying to secure the fertile floodplains of Punjab and end their own agricultural woes back home. Administration of the refugee camps required that hundreds of professionals leave their regular jobs and work out of makeshift tents. The cost of such disruptions to Pakistan's economy was not lost on MCOs like Kifayat Ali. If he took pride in doing something for the community, he was also aware that the rural banking effort might just be indispensable to national survival.

As Ali negotiated the curving roads outside Peshawar, I was reeling from the jolt of rocks under the wheels. He weaved past mules and bullock-drawn carts carrying the cuttings of newly harvested sugar and wheat. Occasionally the road penetrated orchards that filled the nostrils with scents of persimmon, plum, and apple blossoms. Workers along the banks of a huge irrigation canal harvested red carrot-shaped radishes. "Grown with the help of ADBP loans," Ali shouted. The workers, recognizing the arrival of an MCO, held up their produce like trophies. "What Nishtar has really done," said Ali, "is to replace a paper relationship between bankers and farmers with a *people* relationship. In the old days, a farmer needing credit had to come to the city, complete a form, then be contacted by mail. Most farmers simply didn't take out loans or refused to repay. Now I know my clients personally and watch their progress. It's much more satisfying this way, and their loans get repaid."[4]

When we reached the outermost farm on Ali's route, the bank's regional manager was waiting. M. Azam Khan had been doing business in the area. If he was a typical bank manager in the frontier region, his looks certainly gave no such indication. Like Jamil Nishtar, he had been born and raised in the frontier region, an Urdu-speaking Pathan. But unlike the brown-eyed, dark-complected Nishtar, Khan was fair, his eyes green. His ruddy cheeks, blond hair, and red mustache looked more characteristic of the British colonial commanders who once ruled these parts. "Even people in my own neighborhood need to be convinced that I was born here in the frontier," he quipped. "They take one look at my blond hair, assume I'm a foreigner, then hear me speak Urdu and ask where I learned it. I explain that I've spoken it all my life, that I'm full-blooded Pathan. I suppose only my mother knows for sure."

If he didn't look the physical prototype of a branch bank manager on the northwest frontier, Khan had nevertheless developed a reputation as a steady, level-headed administrator. "I can't idealize this work," he said, as we walked across the fields examining tubewells bought with ADBP loans. "It's terribly hard to make the MCO scheme work out here, though we're doing it, and with some success. In addition to giving credit, we make other services available to the farmers—information, know-how, supplies. Credit is hard enough by itself to deliver. For farmers to make profits, they also need inputs, and information about using them. Nishtar's concept is that you couple credit with education and services—and even do some advocacy with local authorities on behalf of farmers."[5]

Kifayat Ali opened his knapsack and produced several exhibits—the "pass book" required for farmers to register with the government, the ADBP loan application form, and the accounting books.[6] Azam Khan read the surprise on my face. "You're right," he said, "there are a lot of technicalities; the accounting itself takes enormous effort. But here again, we're making things more efficient through computerizing the system. Nishtar is computerizing everything. We're also using video technology to help MCOs spread news about innovations. By filming farmers who have good ideas, we can cross-pollinate whole regions. It may seem a high price to pay for bringing disadvantaged farmers into the world of commerce and ideas. But we're seeing payoffs. And that keeps us going."[7]

■

With his MCO system Nishtar had by no means abandoned the concept of a strong centralized organization, though the new farmer-centered orientation was a decentralization of sorts. The whole structure of ADBP now had an outward service orientation it never had before. The MCO functioned as much farmer's agent and advisor as officer of the bank. The information-sharing system gave farmers far greater options for action. Access to information was coming to be seen almost as a natural right. Meanwhile the system legitimized and encouraged the flow of ideas and complaints from farmers back to the system. Nishtar himself made it a point to leave the office regularly, get out to the fields, and talk with farmers.[8] In fact, he insisted that the idea of the MCO originated through such dialogue at the grassroots. As a managerial style, Nishtar's effort to maintain dialogue with "people at the bottom" radically separated him from his predecessors.

When it came to positioning his bank in relation to national and international power, Nishtar had to play an equally sophisticated game. As head of an institution that was part of the national banking system, Nishtar was still directly responsible to political leaders, and in a martial law administration this would prove restrictive for a man of change. In a constantly expanding bank, new infusions of money would also be needed, much of it from the international community. Again, the climate of world policies would greatly shape the context in which the new banking concept must survive. Positioning and repositioning his bank in relation to this macro-politics was a game Nishtar particularly relished. But exactly how he played the game, I was still not clear. In the mid-1980s I had begun piecing together perspectives from officials at the World Bank, from the International Fund for Agricultural Development (IFAD) in Rome, and now from Nishtar's own colleagues in the government.[9] What began to emerge was a picture of a man constantly sizing up the global economy, testing its shifting weather, then trying to discern in the storms and sunshine opportunities to strengthen his bank and the farmers it served. To understand, one had to see Nishtar's moves in the flow of history. My notes read almost like headlines from a newspaper story file:

1973

Food crisis hits West Africa and Bangladesh. Starvation threatens hundreds of thousands, the international community is caught off-guard. Emergency aid cannot avert disaster. The horror that follows evokes massive international response.

World Bank president recognizes rural development. Robert S. McNamara rallies his bank and the world financial community to invest more in small farmers, most of them passed up by urban industrial growth.

World's agriculture ministers convene World Food Conference in Rome. Multination programs are launched to prevent future crises and strengthen Third World agriculture.

Oil-rich OPEC states join with Western nations to start a fund for small-scale agriculture. The International Fund for Agricultural Development, based in Rome, invests in the poorest countries.[10]

Mid-1970s

Economic planners in Pakistan worry over smallholders. New study shows number of small farms on the rise. Pakistani fathers continue the Muslim tradition of dividing land among sons.[11]

Three quarters of Pakistani farmers with small farms are getting only 10 percent of nation's bank credit. Ironically, small farms are more productive per acre than large farms that get the lion's share of credit.[12] Central Bank chairman Jamil Nishtar suspects small farmers could increase productivity two or three times, given better credit and inputs.

1977

Unexpected shortfall: Pakistan imports 2.5 million tons of wheat. The nation could be self-sufficient, but production lags. As rural economy declines, more rural people migrate to cities.

Urban investment up 6 percent: Rural banking in shambles. Repayment rates are low. Inefficiencies discourage World Bank from making new loans to Pakistan.

Soviet Union invades Afghanistan. Millions of refugees spill into northwest Pakistan. Economic pressures intensify and the political mandate rises to invest more in the countryside.

International bankers more sympathetic to Pakistan's plight. Central Bank chairman Nishtar argues the time is ripe—at home and abroad—to improve rural banking.

1978–79

Nishtar takes helm of Agricultural Development Bank of Pakistan. ADBP launches new system of "Mobile Credit Officers." Justifies giving small farmers more credit and information as a way to improve bank efficiency and loan repayment.[13]

ADBP gets backing from international banks. Impressed with Nishtar's plan, the World Bank, IFAD, and the Asian Development Bank back Nishtar with 55 billion rupees in loans, promising more as ADBP grows.

1980–81

Reagan administration takes office, stresses free enterprise as the engine for world economic growth. The new American administration urges tilt in the policies of the international banks. World Bank presses governments of poor countries to support free markets and reduce governmental control.

New strings attached to World Bank contracts with ADBP. World Bank planners want higher percentages of ADBP loans to reach small farms. Encourage Pakistani government to relieve ADBP from regulations impeding business efficiency. A delighted Jamil Nishtar takes advantage.[14]

1982–83

Rural development gains higher priority in Pakistan. Leading World Bank economist appointed Minister of Planning in Pakistan. Mahbub ul Haq believes Pakistan can become the "new South Korea," with agricultural exports powering national growth.[15] Nishtar takes advantage, presses for new expansion of ADBP.

ADBP lending approaches level of commercial banks. Nishtar's corps of 717 MCOs reaches 18,000 of Pakistan's 35,000 "reachable" villages, lending 1,370 million rupees. High-tech communications to give farmers access to vital information.

ADBP contracts with Japanese for farm machinery and video. Asian Development Bank, supported by Japan, gives ADBP $10 million loan to import tractors from Japan. Nishtar sees further opportunity, persuades Japanese government to include communications equipment.

Mid-1980s

ADBP lending to small farmers reaches all-time high. Loans to small farmers now over half the agricultural total, compared to 10 percent in 1978. Five billion rupees are being disbursed, compared to only one billion in 1978. Nearly 1,200 MCOs are reaching farmers in all 35,000 villages considered viable for banking.

Agricultural loan recovery hits all-time high. Repayment reaches 90 percent, compared to only 54 percent in 1979. Nishtar seeks to extend MCO system further. Hundreds of thousands of farm families are benefiting; Nishtar believes many more of the nation's four million farm families could be reached.[16]

■

Nishtar's offer to meet again was an invitation I could not refuse. As I entered his office, it was late morning. He had still not returned from his daily ritual of hand-picking new MCOs from a pool of the country's top agricultural graduates. This hands-on approach, while it had attracted admiration, had also drawn criticism. Some who had watched Nishtar over the years felt he was asserting a personal control over the system that verged on the autocratic.[17] As he walked into the office, pipe in hand, Nishtar resumed our conversation as if it had never stopped. "I hope you're seeing how impressive these

MCOs are," he said. "With the MCO system now in place, all kinds of new innovations are becoming possible. We're extending the MCO concept in new directions. We'll have what I call the *functional* MCO—providing assistance for dairying, poultry, irrigation, and other activities.[18] We're starting to send out husband-and-wife teams, MCO couples. This makes it possible for women to get involved, and it means more bank credit will go to women. And we'll greatly expand the use of high-tech communications. I want you to understand my philosophy about this."

Nishtar never left philosophy out of his explanations. He rose, walked around the desk, and invited me to move to some armchairs near a window overlooking the city. "You see, I'm not an intermediate technology man. In this I differ from economists who say that underdeveloped countries should opt for low- or intermediate-level technologies—Fritz Schumacher's view in *Small Is Beautiful.* In my view, we need the highest possible technology that is appropriate for the situation. When it comes to communications, that means we should bring to the service of farmers the top-flight technologies—satellites, computers, TVs—in the most extensive way possible. The potential for education is enormously enhanced and our bank management gets much more efficient."

In this Nishtar was a manager's manager, a technocrat's technocrat. And he had considerable reason for believing what techno-managerial efficiency can do. But I couldn't help wondering if his bent for managerial control, for the technological fix and the banker's bottom line, would eventually outrun his conviction that people should be freed to achieve their own goals. I put caution aside: "How do you respond, Mr. Chairman, to those who say that your management is hampered by a top-down quality, a tendency to be too controlled, too centralized, too determined from above?"[19] Nishtar paused. "There *are* a lot of misconceived top-down ventures which only line the pockets of bureaucrats, and leave people at the bottom with little chance to benefit or get involved," he said. "But if you conceive your model well enough, you can overcome the dangers. It's not really a question of taking *either* a top-down *or* a bottom-up approach, *either* a controlled *or* a liberating approach. You've got to have *both.* You need to enable people in the countryside to realize what they want to do. Unless they *want* a program and are involved in its design, nothing will happen; the program will collapse. On the other hand, you've got to be realistic about the support rural change needs at the national and global levels. You need to persuade government to put in place policies favorable to rural growth. And to do that you've got to have in place real organizational strength and central managerial expertise. Otherwise your efforts won't gain the confidence of government or the world community. It's a balance—accountability below, accountability above. This is really what the MCO concept is about."

■

The passing of a reformer can be followed by continuation or collapse of reform. Only time will tell, and the intentions of the reformer's successors are always decisive. From all early indications, the untimely death of Jamil Nishtar in 1987 did not end the reforms he had begun. Small farmers all over Pakistan continued to take out loans from the MCOs Nishtar himself had hired and trained. Bank lending continued to grow, MCOs to innovate.

"It seems the charisma has not passed away with the man," I said, pouring myself more tea at the Harvard Square Cafe. Dick Goldman nodded. "The style of leaders like Nishtar sometimes makes them folk heroes during their own lifetime," he said. "But occasionally their ideas seem to persist after they're gone, and that makes you think there was something behind the leadership style that had validity in itself. You may not be able to quantify that style for economic analysis. But in the life context it makes a huge economic difference."

1. On the role in Iran's revolution played by neglect of the rural economy, see Richard M. Harley, "Food: Humanity's Need, America's Interest" (*The Christian Science Monitor*, March 6, 1981), pp. 12–13.

2. This approach was typical of development strategies in many countries during the 1950s and 1960s. In Africa, for instance, a World Bank study states that "While part of [the borrowing done in that period] was used to maintain consumption when commodity prices fell . . . most of [it] went to finance large public investments, many of which contributed little to economic growth or to generating foreign exchange to service the debt. These projects covered a wide spectrum of sectors and countries. Examples include projects such as large conference centers, administrative buildings, university centers, hotels, and highways, as well as projects in the industrial sector, such as oil and sugar refineries, steel mills, and textile and cement factories. They occurred in low-income countries as well as in middle-income countries and most oil exporters. . . . Too many projects have been selected either on the basis of political prestige or on the basis of inadequate regard for their likely economic and financial rate of return. . . . External financial agencies have shared the responsibility for this inadequate discipline over the use of investment resources" ("Toward Sustained De-

)

velopment in Sub-Saharan Africa: A Joint Program of Action" [Washington, DC: International Bank for Reconstruction and Development/The World Bank, 1984], p. 24).

3. A prerequisite for the emergence of ADBP's Mobile Credit Officer system was the existence of a large pool of unemployed college graduates, most with agricultural degrees. According to Jamil Nishtar, any replication of the MCO concept in other countries would require a similar large reserve of unemployed, educated youth. "This you would not find in most African countries. But you might find it in a country like Nigeria, or the Asian countries of India, Bangladesh, and Indonesia" (Interview, April 1987, Islamabad).

4. The personal connection was one of many incentives Nishtar built into the system to sustain the commitment of MCOs—incentives that compared quite favorably with those of the previous rural banking system. MCOs were paid much more than earlier rural bank workers, were granted ownership of their motorcycles, and served full-time rather than the half-time generally prevailing in the previous system. And the simple requirement that the bankers-on-bikes be graduates of agricultural colleges meant that the personal background of the new generation of bank workers gave them a much stronger interest in serving farmers and farmer interests. Previously, most bank workers had been semieducated, retired military officers, with much less direct personal concern for the farm community.

5. Early in his term as ADBP chief, Nishtar became convinced that MCOs would have to do more than provide credit and information, and actually be public advocates on behalf of their clients. Without such advocacy, farmers would not be assured of the public services they needed to translate loans into profits, and to pay back the bank. In the Lahore area in 1980, for example, a growing number of farmers were taking out ADBP loans to install electric-powered deep tubewells. Because electric power was generally available in the area, farmers had every expectation of being able to operate their tubewells. But utility officials proved reluctant to provide service to one subregion. When the local MCO learned of the problem, he visited the utility office to see if something could be done. His arguments were persuasive. After a few months the service was installed, and his client farmers could install and operate their tubewells. The effectiveness of such public advocacy eventually led Nishtar to formalize its role in regular MCO responsibilities. MCOs became obligated "to maintain liaison with public and private agencies dealing with inputs and service supplies," and "to identify the crop marketing channel, and to co-ordinate activities with such channels for obtaining better prices and in collection of sale proceeds" (Shama Rehman, "Mobile Credit Officers Monitoring Report" [Islamabad: ADBP, 1982], p. 3).

6. In many countries these documents have been passports to greater opportunity for farmers, but for less-advantaged, illiterate peasants they have often proved a barrier. In the late 1970s in northwest Pakistan, for instance, farmers were required to go to the post office in the city of Peshawar to get their "pass book." Many complained that—apart from the inconvenience of the travel—they were confronted on arrival with a 50-rupee fee—45 rupees more than the price listed in regulations. Nishtar's branch managers eased the problems by restoring the 5-rupee price and by making it possible for the farmers to secure the book at their own farms through the MCO. Meanwhile, the standard loan application forms in national banks had always been long documents, often requiring detailed information about landholdings and previous loans from other institutions that was not always easy to provide—especially for poorer illiterate farmers. ADBP reduced the length of the form, and MCOs assisted the farmers in completing the forms at home.

7. From a banking standpoint, the outlay of loans and collection of repayments were greatly enhanced by the MCO system. The period of growth from 1979 to 1985,

for instance, totally changed the picture of rural banking. The number of MCOs rose from 14 (serving only 288 of Pakistan's 40,000 villages) to 1,170 (serving 35,176). The percentage of agricultural credit going to smaller farmers (defined as cultivating less than 25 acres) increased from only 29 percent in 1979 to 69 percent in 1985. The rate of loan recovery nationwide improved consistently over the same period. In 1979 recovered loans amounted to only 444.6 million rupees, while in 1985 the figure was 2,252.7 million—nearly five times as great. The fraction of the total amount of outstanding loans that was recovered also greatly increased, from 36.3 percent in 1979 to 73 percent in 1985 (Planning Department, "25 Years of ADBP, 1961–1986, Activities and Achievements" [Islamabad: ADBP, 1986], pp. 16, 17, 33). Meanwhile the unrecovered fraction of the total loan portfolio fell, from 32.2 percent in 1979 (some years before it had been running as high as 52 percent) and 38.8 percent in 1980, to 25.5 percent in 1981, 21.1 percent in 1982, and 17.6 percent in 1983. By 1984 the figure was only 9.5 percent (Interview, April 1987, with Abdul Salam, Chief of the Credit Division). These figures do not reflect loan recovery results in more difficult periods. For instance, when blight devastated cotton production in southern Pakistan in 1983–84, ADBP gave major repayment extensions to hard-hit farmers, and recovery rates for cotton-related loans were only 10–20 percent. But even then, the MCO system made it possible to get better than expected loan repayment, according to studies by ADBP's Credit Division. The target total recovery sought in 1983–84 was 160 crores rupees (one crore = 100,000); some 165 crores were actually recovered.

8. Nishtar recounted one such instance from the early days of developing the MCO concept. He had worried about corruption of the occasional wayward MCO—a distinct possibility, since MCOs would be operating alone in the countryside—and asked farmers themselves how to prevent MCOs from succumbing to favoritism or bribery. The farmers urged a solution that Nishtar adopted as a central characteristic of MCO operations: No loans would be deliberated in isolation from the village as a whole. As Nishtar recalled, one elder farmer in a Punjabi village said, "We normally conduct business matters here in sight of the whole community. If agreements on the loans are made openly before a village community, it would be assured that an MCO would have to treat everyone fairly" (Interview, April 1987, with A. Jamil Nishtar). Nishtar was also convinced that regular input from local farmers was essential if bank procedures were to be suitably adapted to peculiar local needs. "In dealing with agricultural development, one should be very careful not to impose a rigid uniformity. Your geographical and cultural conditions will differ widely. You have a generally universal basis for operating, but you modify your approach for each area" (Interview, April 1987). Early in the MCO scheme, for instance, Nishtar received a complaint from MCOs in the Punjab area that their motorcycles were too big. MCOs in the Baluchistan region, on the other hand, thought their motorcycles were too small. The MCOs in Punjab said they needed smaller cycles because roads became muddy during the rainy season, and bikes occasionally had to be picked up and carried over impassable ground. Also, all Punjabi villages served by MCOs were within a 4 or 5 mile radius, so small bikes were adequate. In contrast, Baluchistan received little rain to make roads muddy, and some villages were as much as 80 or 100 miles apart, so the greater speed and stability of larger, heavier bikes were desirable for traveling long distances. Nishtar responded with appropriately sized motorbikes for each region.

9. Interviews, April 1987, with Dr. Sartaj Aziz, Director of Agricultural Research, and Dr. Mahbub ul Haq, Pakistan's Minister of Planning.

10. On the establishment of the International Fund for Agricultural Development,

see Richard M. Harley, "Setting Aside Politics to Help the Poor," *The Christian Science Monitor*, June 11, 1981, p. B22.

11. The average size of farms in 1970 was 13.5 acres; by 1980 it had dropped to 10 acres, according to Minister of Planning Mahbub ul Haq (Interview, April 1987). A "small farm" in Pakistan is generally defined as a plot of land under 25 acres (about 10 hectares), more strictly under 12.5 acres (about 5 hectares). Official agricultural statistics do not give a breakdown of landholdings smaller than 12.5 acres. For most developing countries, 12.5 acres is quite large as a small-farm designation. A more typical definition of a "small" farm is in the range of 5 acres. Planning Minister Mahbub ul Haq expressed his hope that the Pakistani government would reduce the definition to that level and "give more attention to the really small man, particularly as the land size diminishes even more in the years ahead. But even if we can get good emphasis on the 5 hectare man, we will be quite happy about that."

12. Widely agreed among agricultural economists (see note 13, Chapter Two), although the reasons behind the relative inefficiency of larger farms can differ from country to country. Jamil Nishtar explained one reason pertaining to Pakistan: "The big landlords are generally absentee landlords. They are exploiters, living off the labor of tenant farmers. Generally these landlords do not invest very much in their farms. They don't try to be competitive. Just the opposite is true for smaller farmers. They both own and manage their lands, and they have great incentives for managing efficiently" (Interview, April 1987). According to Minister of Planning Mahbub ul Haq, "All the studies conducted in the Planning Commission show that productivity of the small farmer is higher than the large farmer in Pakistan, particularly higher than the largest. The middle farmer is quite efficient, the 50 to 75 acres fellow. He can use tractors, and is generally open to new ideas in technology. But the farmers above 100 acres are generally absentee landlords. Their productivity per hectare compares very unfavorably in study after study. And when it comes to the repayment of agricultural loans, the rate is much higher for the small farmer than the big landlords, who try to find ways to evade payment. We have over 92 percent recovery from the small farmer. They do not complain over repayment because they are very productive" (Interview, April 1987).

13. The costs of fielding MCOs were, in fact, easily justified in terms of loan repayments and the more effective uses to which the loans were put with the guidance of agriculturally trained MCOs. In 1985, a study of ADBP's supervised credit system noted that servicing 10 to 25 villages with one MCO was cheaper than with bank branches. The maximum annual cost of an MCO was 50,000 rupees (including salary, petrol charges, and depreciation of a motorcycle). Since an MCO servicing 25 villages would have a base lending target of 0.2 million rupees per village every two years, at the end of two years he would be generating and supervising a loan portfolio of 5 million rupees (25 villages at 0.2 million rupees each). The 50,000 rupees needed for an MCO to supervise the credit transactions during the third year would thus amount to only one percent of the loan portfolio. Since the MCO continued to extend loans, the relative cost of his own labor falls even further over time. For MCOs lending in fewer villages, the percentage could be higher, but would still be less than 5 percent of the funds being generated (Rana Shabbir Ahmed Khan, "Supervised Agricultural Credit System in Pakistan" [Islamabad: ADBP, 1985], pp. 21–23).

14. Of particular concern to the World Bank was a requirement by the Pakistani government that ADBP give financial aid at times of emergency need around the country, which would not be repaid. Fearing that this would adversely affect the business self-sufficiency of ADBP in the long run, the World Bank eventually made its

own loans to ADBP contingent on the government's lifting the requirement. World Bank contracts also required 75 percent of ADBP loans go to farmers working less than 25 acres, half of that amount going to farmers working less than 12.5 acres. Nishtar, though not wanting strings of any sort attached to loans from international banks, determined that he could still play the "World Bank card" to his advantage. As he explained to a team of World Bank evaluators: "Ultimately I don't really need the World Bank in order to make ADBP succeed. But I've decided to continue accepting your loans. There are three reasons. First, those loans do come in the form of dollars, and the government needs the foreign exchange. Second, in some cases we can learn a few things from you. And third, sometimes your involvement means I can get things from the government I couldn't otherwise." In fact, Nishtar found the World Bank's contractual emphasis on small farmers and its encouragement of less government interference quite helpful for ADBP (Interview, December 1989, with Joseph Duester, World Bank).

15. The twin objectives of Planning Minister Mahbub ul Haq during the 1982–83 period were (a) to encourage the conversion of subsistence farming into commercially profitable farming, even for smaller farmers, and (b) to give small farmers more control over the means of production (Interview, April 1987). Several steps were encouraged by the Planning Commission under his direction: first, massive new investment in electrification and services for the countryside; second, boosting the prices farmers would receive for their produce, previously only 50 or 60 percent of world prices, to nearly the full world price. Newspapers during this period marked the continued rise of national support for improved opportunities for small farmers. For instance, an editorial appearing in the Pakistani *Morning News* on October 30, 1983, said that, as a result of the encouragement of new incentives for small farmers, the nation's agricultural production had not only achieved self-sufficiency in wheat but also enabled the country to export. However, the paper noted, the cost of production was still a major problem for lower-income small farmers. It argued that the poorest 50 percent of farmers should be the principal beneficiaries of new farm credit incentives to boost agricultural output.

16. The role of international aid in helping Pakistan, and most South Asian countries, to get their agricultural feet on the ground is now well attested. In the late 1980s, the prospects of such assistance undergirding economic growth in troubled Africa were not nearly so bright. In a typical example of many news articles, James Brooke of *The New York Times* reported in July 1987 that, at a time when African countries were making policy changes more favorable to free market conditions, the international finances needed to support those changes were drying up. "Paradoxically, American aid to Africa is leveling off or dropping at a time when Africa is moving toward the most pro-Western economic policies since independence. . . . Some African and Western economists fear that the high cost of servicing the debt [incurred by those African nations] will discredit free market policies in the eyes of many Africans." The article cited the internal strains on countries like Zambia and Ivory Coast which, with the tightening of international financial resources, were faced with a dilemma: Retrench on market-oriented policy reforms and renege on debt repayments, or face riots and internal strife (*New York Times*, July 19, 1987, Section 3, p. 12). Pakistan's Minister of Planning Mahbub ul Haq argued that the Asian experience should encourage an international climate more favorable to investment in long-term development, including increased foreign aid (See note 14, Chapter Two).

17. The World Bank's Joseph Duester was charged for many years with the over-

sight of loans by his bank to ADBP and had many dealings with Jamil Nishtar. The ADBP chairman, according to Duester, tended to keep his distance from his top management people, made decisions without much discussion, and did not tolerate a great deal of criticism. "In the Pakistani context, this style of management may have been appropriate," said Duester in an interview with the author in December 1989, "because ADBP is a hierarchy of civil servants, many of whom end up in their positions just by the years of service, not necessarily their merits. Nishtar's autocratic style might not be right in the United States or Germany, but it may have been the only way to move the bureaucracy in Pakistan."

18. The functional MCOs represented a move on the part of ADBP to diversify lending for items other than tractors. The extent to which ADBP loans were invested in tractors has been controversial, some analysts arguing that the country would profit more from investing in other things. For instance, after studying agricultural policy and performance over the period of 1960 to 1985, Harvard agricultural economist Richard Goldman concluded that government subsidies for tractor purchases primarily favored larger farms by enabling them to substitute machinery for labor. The impact on increasing crop yields had actually been negligible, he argued, as indicated by many studies in India and Pakistan (such as Hans P. Binswanger, *The Economics of Tractors in South Asia* [New York: Agricultural Development Council, 1978], p. 73). And by encouraging machine substitution for labor, the tractor subsidy may have contributed to declining rural wages between 1960 and 1975. "There is no apparent national objective which is served by the subsidy on tractors," Goldman concluded. "It is probably better to let farmers respond to private market incentives in this area and to use scarce public resources to target on inputs which help small farmers disproportionately, such as smaller tubewells" (Interview, July 1989, Harvard Institute for International Development, Cambridge, MA). ADBP, for its part, has attempted to reduce the percentage of its lending that goes for tractor purchase. In 1979 tractor loans comprised 74 percent of the ADBP portfolio. By 1984 it was down to 69 percent, by 1985 to 59 percent. By 1989—Nishtar had by then passed away—it was down to 36 percent, while nontractor loans were up to 64 percent (*Annual Report, Agricultural Development Bank of Pakistan* [Islamabad: ADBP, 1989]).

19. Debate over "top-down" vs. "bottom-up" approaches to rural development has sometimes centered on concern about the ability of the rural poor to "participate" in the planning and execution of programs supposed to benefit them. One school of thought takes what might be called an "inducement" standpoint. It tries to find ways to *induce* greater participation in order to achieve better program results. Another school takes what might be called an "empowerment" standpoint. It argues for more open-ended approaches to program design, conceived on the basis of evolving aspirations of the rural peoples themselves, and stresses the enhancement of community capacities so that communities can seize their own destiny. The former school tends to see the participation issue from the standpoint of planners/managers, their need to carry out program objectives and to deal efficiently with the "target" populations involved (see John M. Cohen & Norman T. Uphoff, "Participation's Place in Rural Development," *World Development*, Vol. 8, 1980, pp. 213–235). The latter, or empowerment, school tries to see the issue more from the perspective of local peoples, those who are supposed to "participate" (Rudi Klauss & David C. Korten, *People-Centered Development: Contributions toward Theory and Planning Frameworks* [West Hartford, CT: Kumarian Press, 1984]; Guy Gran, *Development by People: Citizen Construction of a Just World* [New York: Praeger, 1983]; Dennis Goulet, "Development as Liberation: Policy Lessons from Case Studies," *World Development*, Vol.

7, 1979, pp. 555–566). In a paper prepared by this writer for the United Nations Food and Agriculture Organization, I argued that some framework involving a *combination* of inducement and empowerment perspectives may be more useful than one that regards them as mutually exclusive. To be sustained over time, the participatory aspects of a program will have to look good to *both* national planners (the inducers) and beneficiaries (those being empowered)—a mutually beneficial arrangement considered by both as in their interest and worth the costs. When planner or participant feels that the benefits are becoming inadequate and the costs too high, a new equilibrium will have to be devised or the program abandoned (Richard M. Harley, "Lessons of Country Experiences: Effective Participation of Small Farmers and Landless in Rural Development, Practical Implications and Limitations" [Cambridge, MA: Mimeo. presented to the United Nations FAO, April 1985], pp. 1–5).

5

Excursion to Economic Extremity:
How Unreachable Are
the "Unreachable Poor"?

TANGAIL, BANGLADESH

In rural society no persons are more economically powerless than those who own no land, especially unmarried or widowed women. Traditionally the landless have survived by doing odd jobs, or by working for people who do own land. And policy makers have seldom given the landless a central place in their plans for rural investment. The lion's share of national bank loans have gone to landholders; people with no land or collateral were assumed too great a risk. In Bangladesh, such policies and assumptions held little promise for the landless poor—more than half the population. A new bank, the Grameen (rural) Bank, set out to prove the common assumptions wrong.

We reached the bus terminal fifteen minutes late. Muzammel Huq was not worried. "This is Bangladesh time," he said, pointing to a vehicle still boarding passengers. He led the way into the crowded bus and found two empty seats toward the back. Legroom was short. My knees pressed uncomfortably against the seat in front. Fortunately the window could be opened to let in the morning breeze. Outside, street vendors held tangerines up to the window, tempting us to buy. We did. More minutes ticked by. "When does the bus leave?" I asked. "When it's full," smiled Muzammel. People kept crowding on board, placing makeshift seats down the center aisle until the vehicle was packed shoulder to shoulder, five and six

65

across. Never had a window seat looked so beautiful. The driver finally revved up the motor, stripped the gears, and launched his heavy-ladden vessel into a sea of morning traffic.

"Have you heard of Pakistan's system of bankers on motorbikes?" I asked Muzammel Huq, who was helping to direct a different rural banking scheme in Bangladesh. "It's a huge advance for Pakistan," he said. "But the scheme has one very unfortunate element. You see, it's based on the idea that there are two classes of poor people in the rural areas—some you can reach with loans, others you cannot. The first they call *viable,* the second *nonviable.*" Muzammel grinned at the thought, then puffed his cigarette and blew smoke into the air. "To be viable," he said, "you have to own 10 to 25 acres of land and have a reputation for being entrepreneurial, progressive. To be nonviable, on the other hand, means that you own little or no land and are thought so disadvantaged that you're beyond economic hope. People like this are not deemed worthy of credit. They are the nonviable. The problem, of course, is that many able farmers get excluded from the credit they need—not to mention the landless, who don't qualify at all. In our country over 50 percent of our hundred million people are landless.[1] Are you going to exclude them from all opportunity? Wait until their numbers, and frustrations, grow even more? And only then try to recover? Here in Bangladesh we cannot accept this idea of a viable and nonviable poor."[2]

I flipped through my notebook to the comments of Pakistan's agricultural bank chairman Jamil Nishtar. He did indeed subscribe to the existence of a nonviable poor. "From the banker's point of view," Nishtar had said, "you have to identify the right man, the farmer who has the desire to improve himself, has integrity, is progressive. To the poorest and landless you must not give loans. You may give them charity, but not loans. In every culture there are people like this who are not productive. In our country it's 5 to 10 percent, in Bangladesh 50 percent. There's nothing you can do about them."

Muzammel smiled. "In our bank," he said, "we've shown that landless people are not bad banking prospects at all. In fact, they're far *more* reliable than the wealthier landowners who take out loans. Grameen Bank has proved this without question." The bus continued to make its way north from Dhaka, the Bangladeshi capital. Our destination was the city of Tangail, a five-hour drive to the north. There I hoped to take a closer look at how Grameen

Bank was making credit available to landless people. By reputation, at least, the experiment had found a way to make loans to people with no collateral and the bank to get its money back. This was not the only experiment of its kind, but one of the more successful.[3] By the late 1980s its model of rural credit was being adapted not only for other areas in Asia but in Africa and also in North America. Programs were being tested for the benefit of Native Americans in Oklahoma, Minnesota, and Ontario, for declining small towns in Arkansas, as well as for the inner-city poor in cities like Chicago and Toronto.

Grameen Bank had come a long way since 1975 when Muhammad Yunus, an economics professor, laid the foundation by lending his own pocket money to the landless poor near Chittagong University in southeast Bangladesh. Anyone with an income-earning venture could qualify—rickshaw pullers, bicycle repairmen, traders hawking all kinds of goods and services. In the beginning Yunus simply wanted to know if borrowers would repay their loans. They *did*, he found, when conditions were right. He expanded in the Chittagong district under the wing of the national banks. By 1983 he had fully tested his model in the south-central district of Dhaka and got permission from the government to operate as an independent bank. Funding for expansion came from the International Fund for Agricultural Development, based in Rome.[4] By 1987 Grameen Bank was reaching 6,000 villages in 6 of the country's 64 districts, with 335 branches and 300,000 borrowers; by the end of 1988 it had about 500 branches serving 10,000 villages. The target was 17,000 branches by 1995. Loan repayment was exceeding 95 percent, according to bank records. Most striking, in the social context of Bangladesh, three quarters of the loans went to the most economically vulnerable of villagers—women.

Our bus pressed on toward Tangail, passing field after field of newly planted rice and vegetables. Cropping patterns made a patchwork quilt of the flat landscape. Some plots shimmered with silver waters, their mirror-smooth surface pierced by the tips of young green rice shoots; others were green with densely packed rows of vegetables or stunningly yellow with fulminations of flowering mustard. In the distance, a cluster of trees cradled a stone mansion with dome-crested turrets, arched colonnades, and exterior stairways leading down to a pond. The now-vacant building had been home to one of the *zamindars*, landlords appointed by British colonial governors to control the countryside and collect taxes to finance the empire.[5]

Bangladeshi civilization had taken root on an extraordinary repository of wetlands off the northeast corner of India. Situated at the mouth of the Ganges and Brahmaputra Rivers, its 26 million acres came to be crisscrossed by 5,000 miles of rivulets and waterways. Farmers could expect yearly replenishment of their lands by these silt-rich streams, some flowing down from Himalayan peaks to the west. During the wet season, from May to September, the country was literally awash with fertility. This, combined with the intense energy of a tropical sun, made conditions ideal for crop cultivation. The poet Rabindranath Tagore once praised his "Bengal of gold" as a land where the fragrance of mango groves can "make a person wild with joy," where "full-blossomed paddy fields spread sweet smiles all over," where the "quilt of harvest spreads at the feet of banyan trees along the riverbanks."

Tagore's Bengal, however, had long suffered a vulnerability to hunger and poverty that seemed to contradict, if not jeer at, its natural abundance. The reasons were many. Torrents rushing down from the neighboring Himalayas, fed by monsoon rains, could wash away what fruits the land brought forth. Other factors were political—the legacy of a bitter and bloody separation from Pakistan in the early 1970s, years of military rule, economic mismanagement and poor planning for flood relief, and the more general concentration of land and wealth in the hands of a relative few.[6] But for such political obstacles, most analysts believed the country could easily have been self-sufficient in food. If the level of rice production could be raised to just one ton per acre, the nation would have enough to feed its people with some left over for export. By the late 1980s, however, only half that goal had been reached. Serious food shortage and poverty remained, to which Grameen Bank was, in part, a response.

"Of course, if you want to open banking to the landless poor—people who are utterly powerless and have little or no collateral—you need a different approach from what you'd do for the owners of land," explained Muzammel Huq. "We at Grameen Bank do not lend to individuals, but to *groups* of borrowers—five-person groups. This is our way of protecting the bank, as well as strengthening the individual borrowers." He pointed to a bank brochure elaborating the point. Group borrowing was a means of protecting bank interests, since borrowers came under pressure from their groups to pay back loans. Borrowers themselves also benefited from group borrowing. If one borrower became ill, the group could keep up his or her loan repayments. In other cases group support could be essential for encouraging a timid member to learn the loan procedure and accept its discipline. "So this group borrowing mechanism has been key to reaching the landless," said Huq. "To reach the more severely disadvantaged, we think you've got to have an alternative approach like this. The fact that it's more difficult to reach the poorest doesn't mean that they're unworthy of loans, or unreachable. It simply means you need an approach that's capable of reaching them, while protecting the bank at the same time. We have no doubt this can be done."[7]

We got off the bus just outside Tangail at a village called Basail. A meeting of women borrowers had just begun. Thirty women were seated cross-legged on mats spread across the ground in a shaded clearing. Barefoot, bare-chested children looked on from the doors and windows of bamboo huts. "This is a borrowers' organization we call a Center," said Muzammel Huq. "It's comprised of six five-person groups, and meets every week. The weekly meeting allows our bank agents to keep in touch with borrowers and collect regular loan repayments. For many women borrowers these meetings are their first encounter with participatory democracy. They elect a new chairperson for their Centers each year."[8]

Seated at the front of the Center, facing the women borrowers, was a young woman banker. Rules of the bank allowed only female bankers to serve women borrowers, male bankers men. Beside the banker knelt a young mother in a bright green sari, clutching a naked baby with her left hand, a bankbook in her right. The baby's eyes, outlined with eye pencil, looked twice their real size. Muzammel Huq asked the woman a question in Bengali, then turned to translate. "Her name is Sharashawti Raj Bengshi," he said. "She's the wife of a village fisherman, mother of four. She inherited a family trade of fishnet making, and has taken out a loan to market her nets more widely around the area. It's brought a nice income for her." The young woman held up a net for Muzammel Huq's inspection. "As you can see," he said, "it's a fine mesh, made with an intricate handwoven technique. Some of these age-old family trades were endangered by the floods of 1974. Fine cloth weaving is another. Our loans help to rejuvenate these trades."

Sharashawti returned to her business with the bank agent, and signed her name on a loan form. Though illiterate, she had learned to write her name as a precondition for taking out loans. The sight of illiterate women transacting business in organized groups was one I had rarely seen in village society. My memory flashed back to a meeting some time before with a young Bangladeshi economist who had come home after finishing doctoral studies in the United States. It was the first time he had witnessed the women of his country taking out loans. "I'm not emotional by nature," he said, "but when I talked with these women I choked up. To believe that, in my own lifetime, I would see illiterate village women, their saris drawn up around their faces, explaining to me, an outsider—a male outsider— how the bank works, when their only way to count is on their ten fingers, and all they can write is their name—I mean, I was taken aback. It's a kind of joy that's hard to explain."[9]

As the fishnet maker returned to her seat among the borrowers, Muzammel Huq conversed in Bengali with another borrower. He turned to translate. "This is Ag Elashin," he said. "Her husband was disabled several years ago. She was left supporting him and three children. She already had some skills making pottery, and now decided to go commercial. With a bank loan she found new ways to market her work in neighboring villages. It's a scenario you'll hear time and again from women in these villages. For one reason or another they've had to become breadwinners, or starve." Muzammel Huq stood up before all the borrowers and asked how many were widows. The majority raised their hands. "You get the point," he said. "But the nice thing about the bank's approach is that there's absolutely no charity involved in helping people like this. European and American agencies have run relief programs here since the floods of 1974; they've given out charitable aid but asked nothing in return. People got dependent on handouts. Grameen Bank, on the other hand, gives out loans to landless people on the condition that they get more productive and repay—including 16 percent interest. It sounds incredible, but their repayment rate is running well over 95 percent."[10]

■

If Grameen Bank was doing much to improve the economic image of the landless poor, it still had not silenced all doubt about their "viability." Some national planners downplayed its promise as a tool for economic growth. If the bank had shown that people at the margin *can* be reached with credit, that did not mean a country like Bangladesh *should* invest scarce resources in quite this way. Bank loans for microenterprise, critics argued, could not make a significant dent in the problem of unemployment and poverty among the swelling ranks of landless people. Of the nation's 55 million landless poor in 1990, Grameen Bank was reaching fewer than 500,000. By the turn of the century the more general challenge of employing the landless would grow even more ominous than it already was. The rural labor force in poor agricultural countries like Bangladesh was expected to double between 1970 and the year 2000, with fewer than 10 percent of the necessary new jobs likely to come from agriculture. Sufficient employment and improved incomes, critics argued, could be generated only by medium- and large-scale industry in the countryside, not the kind of small-scale enterprise supported by Grameen Bank. The Grameen concept had its merits, they admitted. But it should be considered more in the category of welfare, not a serious tool in the kit of national economic planners.[11]

Given such criticism, I quite expected bank workers to counter with a defense of their own. Many rejoinders were possible, since the bank had by now gathered much statistical evidence of what could be done to improve the lot of the landless poor. Bank workers could have charged the critics with failure to recognize what the landless had been able to do, given the chance, or with short-sightedness about what the bank could do further to alleviate poverty, given more national resources. But I heard no such justifications. In fact, they seemed utterly absent from the words of the bank workers, including the Director himself, Muhammad Yunus. Instead, he justified Grameen Bank as a good *business venture.* Providing a service needed by the public, said Yunus, and trying to provide the service at a profit, constitute—purely and simply— good business.

By the late 1980s some analysts were contending that Grameen Bank was surviving as an institution not because it was truly profitable, but because its operations were still subsidized by international agencies and other donors.[12] Whatever the truth about the bank's financial sustainability, Yunus's justification of his bank as "good business" was puzzling. In one sense I could understand his argument perfectly well. The late '80s had brought growing international recognition that private enterprise and free markets must play a major role in boosting economic growth in poor nations. Since Ronald Reagan had come to the American presidency in 1981, political support had been growing in the United States for aid programs that encouraged entrepreneurship, including Grameen-style credit.[13] Policies in developing nations also were coming to be more supportive of entrepreneurial activity, and of programs that promote it.[14] In such a business-friendly international climate, Yunus's "good business" rationale would clearly be persuasive. Yet why did Yunus justify his bank so *exclusively* in business terms? Had he abandoned his original goal of elevating the landless poor on the list of national priorities, demonstrating their human and economic "viability"?

On returning to the capital city of Dhaka, I determined to press the Director in person for the answer. I found him one hot afternoon at the bank's head office. The building—a modest office block on the outskirts of the city—was the antithesis of the high-rise headquarters of the Agricultural Development Bank of Pakistan. Yunus was seated behind a large desk in a dimly lit, scantily furnished office. Slight of build but forceful in speech, he cut a handsome boyish image, accentuated by a shock of wavy black hair. Why, I asked, have you become so adamant about this good-business argument? Surely you do not believe the value of Grameen Bank will be judged by its performance as a business? "We are bankers," he replied. "If you're looking for a movement for social justice, or an institution to ease unemployment and poverty, you need to look elsewhere. Here we give loans, not plans for social reform. I'm not against reform, of course. I'm just saying that our purpose is to be *bankers.* There's a public demand for our services. We seek to make a profit on our lending. Though we take out loans from the national banks, we are not drawing down government resources—in fact, the government makes money from us.[15] So Grameen Bank is justified because it is a business venture that benefits its employees, the people, the government."

For all Yunus's seriousness, his voice carried a hint of tease, as if to admit there was more to his motivation than entrepreneurship. I made a last attempt to draw him out: "Surely you would not deny the humanitarian goals—alleviating poverty, unemployment, showing the economic worth of the poor, and so on?" He yielded no ground. "We try to wear just *one* hat here—the hat of a banker, not social or humanitarian reformer. That would confuse people, espe-

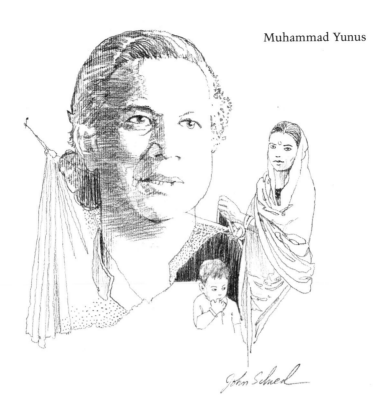

John Schnell

cially our borrowers. They might think we have special goals in mind, and then concoct artificial ideas for loans they think we'd approve. Instead, we say, 'Look, we are bankers. You are people who need to earn a living. You know what you do best. If you need money, talk to us. If we think you'll earn money and repay, we'll give you the loan. You make a profit, we earn interest, we're both better off.' With this approach, the initiative is theirs. It's their project, their planning. *They* must be the ones to initiate and carry through."

Here, then, was at least *some* explanation for the good-business rationale. Beyond claiming for the bank a legitimate place in the economy, it was a way to keep goal setting in the hands of bank borrowers, not the bankers themselves. Still, this did not explain everything. Grameen Bank was unquestionably one of Bangladesh's more visible symbols that the landless poor were worthy of inclusion in national development. Why downplay the social and humanitarian aspects? Could not Yunus permit himself a few moments to celebrate the act of reaching poor people, changing their prospects—

however modestly—for the better? Perhaps he felt the humanitarian benefits spoke well enough for themselves. Perhaps he was tired of debates over which economic strategies do the most to ease poverty. I left his office with only partial explanations, a collection of hunches. That seemed the most I could expect to find—until, that is, I visited a town called Chilmari.

■

Chilmari was, in some ways, the extreme in a land of extremities. Simply getting there was in itself an extremity. From Dhaka in the south-central part of the country, the journey took five hours by bus to the northwest, three hours by ferry up the Brahmaputra River to the city of Rangpur, then two more hours of hot, dusty driving to the east. Life in rural Chilmari seemed to go on in utter remove from the more frenetic urban pace of neighboring Rangpur. Rangpur exhibited a curious blend of national and international influences. Along its narrow winding streets, the shops of Bengali merchants were interspersed with Chinese restaurants, stores selling British bicycles and Japanese motorcycles, and retail outlets for Bridgestone tires (Japanese) and Philips TV (Dutch). The persistence of English as a second language hinted at the depth to which British colonialism had penetrated Bengali culture. English was also a lifeline to the wider world of commerce in South Asia. By contrast to cosmopolitan Rangpur, the tiny village of Chilmari seemed a settlement just off the edge of history, little touched by the winds of commerce or by the "universal language." It was a spread of small one-story stucco structures, surrounded on its outskirts by huts of elaborately woven bamboo and roads leading to villages beyond. Now that the cool of winter had receded, hot dry breezes swept the landscape, stirring a fine white dust into ground-level eddies that intercepted all moving things, including our Land-Rover. To close the car windows was to suffer unbearable heat; to open them was to invite suffocation by dust.

For sheer survival, Chilmari and other outlying villages were built on high ground. Everyone knew that the wet season each year would bring new flooding from rain rushing down from the Himalayas. To ensure the passage of vehicles, roads also were elevated on embankments, some six to ten feet high. In addition to facilitating traffic, the banks trapped water in vast pools ideal for cultivating rice and fish. Occasionally, the floods' angrier moods proved too much for the

banks. In 1974, rising waters repeatedly breached the barriers, wash-
ing away huts and destroying crops. Many thousands died in village
streets or on roads leading to urban centers. In Dhaka the government was slow to respond with relief for the northwest. Only when
starving country folk began to stream into the capital and die in its
streets was the extent of rural crisis taken seriously.[16]

By the time I arrived in Chilmari, where Grameen Bank had established a branch, the village had enjoyed more than a decade of flood-
free years, though few could forget the disaster of '74. The bank's
representative was S. M. Musa, a young college graduate from
Tangail who had come to the area with his wife after serving the
bank in Tangail. "That was child's play compared to here," explained Musa, as we walked through the dusty streets. "We've had
enormous difficulty getting people just to accept the idea of a bank.
The existence of charitable relief agencies in the area made it nearly
impossible even to launch the bank at all." Like many of the college
graduates attracted by the bank, Musa spoke excellent English. His
slacks and trim open-neck shirt distinguished him in appearance
and authority from less-advantaged village men who wore the
skirtlike *lungi* and tattered shirts. "When we first came here several
years ago," he said, "European relief agencies had, for years, been
giving free services in nutrition and health. People got so used to
handouts they couldn't comprehend the idea of taking out a loan and
paying it back *with interest*. We finally got the idea across, but it
wasn't a foregone conclusion."

Making our way to huts on the outskirts of town, we were met by
two women bank workers and Momena Bewa, leader of a local
women borrowers' association. Mrs. Bewa had lost her husband during the 1974 floods. After the first flood hit in June he had tried to
rebuild the family hut. His efforts were decimated by a second flood
in July. When the third flood hit in September he was sick and
exhausted, and died leaving Mrs. Bewa to fend for herself and two
small children. For eight years she roamed from village to village,
trying to eke out a living doing odd jobs. When Grameen Bank came
to the area, she took out a loan and started a business selling household wares. Profits made it possible to put a down payment on a hut.
For the first time in ten years she had an address. Her daughter soon
married the son of a respected village family, and prospects began to
look up.

Why, I asked Mrs. Bewa, had villagers finally embraced the idea of Grameen Bank, when they could have continued to take handouts from charities? "I remember when Dr. Yunus first came and told us about the bank," she said. "We were skeptical. He asked if we remembered the floods of 1974. Yes of course, we said, that was a terrible time, people dying everywhere. Then he asked if any of us had lost relatives. We were quiet. All of us had losses. He asked if we thought the suffering of 1974 would come again. We were still quiet. He said, 'I tell you, the suffering *will* come again, because you are doing nothing to prevent it.' Now that got us thinking. We knew he was right. We had to do more to help ourselves. But what? He told us we could take out loans. 'Expand your businesses,' he said, 'but you must understand the bank's rules and pay back what you borrow. Then you'll be more secure.' We did. Now most all the women in my group are better off. I don't know if we could survive another 1974, but we will have a far better chance."

If Yunus's early work in Chilmari had served to awaken in villagers a desire to reduce dependency and do more for themselves, by now the bank was itself a symbol of reduced dependency in the countryside. I was beginning to think I had my answer about why bank workers, and Yunus himself, shied away from the language of poverty alleviation and welfare. Justifying the bank in those terms would risk having it linked to ideas of charity, which the bank was trying to overcome. The language of "good business" got the message more nearly right, distinguishing the bank from charity or relief. And, in a strange way, it affirmed what Yunus had set out to prove from the outset: To the extent that Grameen Bank proved itself "good business," it would show that the "unviable poor" were not so economically unviable after all. Otherwise the bank would not be able to retrieve its loans, and would cease to exist. Far from an abandonment of his early humanitarian goals, Yunus's good-business rationale was a confirmation of them, and in the most convincing of bottom-line terms. He still had a long way to go to prove that the bank was sustainable; but he had also come a very long way.[17]

That night I boarded a small twin-engine aircraft to return to Dhaka. For one lingering moment the glow of setting sun transformed a land of poverty into the "Bengal of gold" Tagore had once praised. The takeoff of the small plane, had it occurred in any rich country, would have drawn little notice. Here it attracted hundreds of spectators who came from surrounding villages to watch from behind a wire fence. What significance would a venture like Grameen Bank ultimately have for villagers like these—twenty, thirty, forty years hence? In some ways, critics of the bank were probably right: Fuller reductions of rural poverty would require national policy changes that encouraged employment opportunities on a much vaster scale, largely through industries more sophisticated than the tiny microenterprises supported by Grameen Bank.[18] Still, activities like the bank's might be helping to create conditions for such economic expansions to take hold.

Muzammel Huq had argued as much some weeks before. "You have to realize," he had insisted, "that the people we're talking about—the landless poor—have had excruciatingly little opportunity for generation after generation. If you want to help them progress, you cannot bypass the channels of education they need, or push them ahead too fast. There have to be ways for them to develop confidence in themselves and what they can do. That takes time. But once this confidence grows, they get involved in all kinds of activities they might have avoided before. This is the confidence Grameen Bank inspires. What contribution it will ultimately make, we can't say. But we do know it's already unleashing potentials no one expected from people like this. You see it in the intensity of their eyes when they pay back their loans."[19]

1. The problem of landlessness, and the concentration of landholdings, had been growing worse in Bangladesh for decades. A study in 1939 gave early indications of the relative concentration of landholdings, showing that 75 percent of farm households owned 5 acres or less. By 1968 the figure had risen to 83 percent (Mohiuddin Alamgir, *Famine in South Asia* [Cambridge, MA: Oelgeschlager, Gunn & Hain, 1980], p. 107).

2. In the 1970s aid and development agencies placed much greater priority on assisting small farmers in developing countries. Helping them to increase productivity was widely thought indispensable if rural poverty were to be alleviated. But the 1980s brought a recognition of certain shortcomings in the small-farmer emphasis. Increasing productivity on the farm would not necessarily improve income for the landless. By the late 80s, between 20 and 50 percent of all rural laborers in developing countries were thought to earn a living primarily from nonfarm activities (Judith Tendler, "What Ever Happened to Poverty Alleviation?" [Mimeo report prepared for the Ford Foundation, March 1987], pp. 3–4). Some analysts have argued that an essential part of the answer for landlessness in Bangladesh would be land reform that gave them more holdings (e.g., Betsy Hartmann & James Boyce in *Needless Hunger: Voices from a Bangladesh Village* [San Francisco: Institute for Food and Development

Policy, 1979], pp. 17–28, 39). Others contended that, given the dim prospects for land reform under military regimes like that of Bangladesh, alternative strategies are needed to improve *nonfarm* employment opportunities in the countryside, involving rural people themselves in the planning. (A harbinger of this view was a talk by Dr. Satish C. Jha, manager of the Asian Development Bank's Irrigation and Rural Development Dept., at Harvard Institute for International Development, Sept. 23, 1985.)

3. Some highly successful rural banking schemes have also been developed in Indonesia—BKK (Badan Kredit Kecamatan), operating in Central Java under the supervision of the Provincial Development Bank of Central Java, and KUPEDES (General Rural Credit), administered by the Indonesian Peoples' Bank, a large government-owned commercial bank. They do not limit loans so exclusively to borrowers on the bottom 20 percent of the economic ladder as does Grameen Bank. But the Indonesian efforts have successfully reached many in that category, as well as many in the third and fourth deciles of the national economic scale (Interview, October 1988, with Professor Donald Snodgrass of the Harvard Institute for International Development). Unlike Grameen Bank, the Indonesian banks make loans only to individuals and require collateral as a precondition—if not land, a house. The Indonesian scheme requires an annual rate of interest between 25 and 35 percent, compared to 16 percent for Grameen Bank. Most BKK loans are below $60, while most KUPEDES loans fall in the $150–500 range, to avoid the high handling costs of microloans (Tyler S. Biggs, Donald R. Snodgrass, & Pradeep Srivastava, "On Minimalist Credit Programs," Development Discussion Paper No. 331 [Cambridge, MA: Harvard Institute for International Development, March 1990], pp. 1–15). Extensive experimentation with small-business credit has also been carried out in Latin America and the Caribbean through the efforts of Accion International, based in Cambridge, MA, and the Foundation for International Community Assistance (FINCA), based in Tucson, AZ.

4. The International Fund for Agricultural Development (IFAD), based in Rome, played a key role in supporting Grameen Bank during its formative years, allocating some $30 million in support of bank activities from 1981 to 1984. The Fund was set up in 1977 as a specialized agency of the United Nations to increase food production, reduce malnutrition, and alleviate poverty among the world's most neglected rural populations, including smallholder farmers, landless laborers, pastoralists, artisanal fishermen, and poor rural women.

5. The system of *zamindars,* inaugurated by the British in the late 18th century, was abolished in 1950.

6. See Alamgir, op. cit., introductory chapters.

7. Conceivably, Grameen Bank could have opted for a model of lending to larger groups of borrowers, perhaps based on a model of cooperative organization and leadership. But bank officials argue that the poorest of the poor are inevitably shortchanged in such programs, intimidated by working in a framework of larger numbers; better-off members corner the benefits for themselves. In addition, coops cannot supervise what is actually done with the loans. With the small-group, week-by-week repayment scheme, borrowers are encouraged to carry through on the project they agreed to invest in. By comparison with cooperative organization, the small-group model is more akin to what is sometimes called the "pre-cooperative" model—which allows working groups to remain small, teaches people the basics of how organization works, and at the same time gives them some experience participating in it. This model can serve as an intermediate step for eventual involvement in larger organizations.

8. The "up side" of Grameen Bank's system of loan repayment is that borrowers are allowed to repay a small amount each week, rather than all of it at the end of the

loan period. This mechanism is clearly one reason the bank has been so popular. While landless laborers might find it inconceivable to repay a $50 loan all at once, they are comfortable with paying back $1 per week over a one-year period. The "down side" is that the bank must maintain a labor-intensive system of loan collection and meticulous bookkeeping by hand. Week by week, bank officers must meet face to face with borrowers. It might be argued that more efficient methods can, and should, be found. Yet, since Bangladesh has an abundant supply of literate persons interested in becoming bank officers, Grameen Bank finds the system workable.

9. Interview, January 1985, with Mohiuddin Alamgir of the International Fund for Agricultural Development in Rome.

10. Bank officials attribute the high repayment rate to various factors: (1) Interest rates are extremely attractive (16 percent per year, compared to the rates of local moneylenders, which can run as high as 10 percent per week). (2) Since each person's prospect for getting loans depends on the loan repayment record of others in the group, peer pressure urges repayment. (3) Since national banks will not lend at all to people with no collateral, borrowers come to see Grameen Bank as "their own bank" and want to keep it alive. (4) Weekly payments look good compared to the local moneylenders' requirement that whole loans be repaid at once, often at the penalty of seizing land or a homestead. (5) The possible penalties of failure to repay—litigation or loss of homestead—are costly and discourage cheating the system. (6) Since poor people generally receive small loans and make very modest profits—in contrast to large landowners who ask for large loans—they do not become oriented to "milking" the system. In short, poor people's stakes in repaying their loans tend to be very high, while their ambitions and power to cheat the system are low. On the administrative side, the bank's success might be partly explained by what economist Judith Tendler terms its "minimalist" approach to credit—the financing of lower-risk activities, mainly in trade and commerce, rather than the potentially high-risk activities of manufacturing and services. This approach also avoids the longer time required to evaluate larger, more risky investments, and demands less extensive technical or business training for bank agents. To encourage the selection of profitable investments, it relies on the wisdom of peer groups, whose prospects for getting loans depend on the ability of their members to make profits and repay. (A fuller discussion can be found in Judith Tendler, op. cit., pp. 15–35).

11. Interview, February 1987, with Dr. A. H. Sahadat Ullah of the General Economics Division of the Bangladesh Planning Commission. "The bank provides no direction for where its loans will be used," he said. "This means that rural development proceeds helter-skelter, with no linkage to overall national economic goals. The money could probably be invested in more productive, larger-scale industry. In fact, unless we get more industry, better managerial expertise and technology into the countryside, I don't think we'll really stimulate economic vibrancy on a mass scale, or substantially reduce unemployment and poverty." Other reservations were voiced in a study by Mahabub Hossain ("Credit for the Rural Poor: The Experience of Grameen Bank in Bangladesh" [Dhaka: Bangladesh Institute of Development Studies, October 1984], pp. 164–165): "The productivity of labour in the activities pursued by the landless with the Grameen Bank is relatively low, particularly for the manufacturing and processing activities." The report noted that, compared to the average agricultural wage rate of Taka 1.60 per hour, the average hourly wage rate for trading activities supported by Grameen Bank loans was about Taka 1.92, but only 1.27 for manufacturing (cottage industries). While noting the low labor productivity for manufacturing activities, the report conceded that average *yearly* earnings can be higher from these

activities than from farm work, since manufacturing activities enable workers to be employed more days in the year.

12. Tyler S. Biggs, Donald R. Snodgrass, & Pradeep Srivastava, op. cit., pp. 26–27. Biggs et al. argue that the 16 percent interest per annum charged by Grameen Bank and the high cost of administrating bank operations have so far made it impossible for the bank to cover its costs without outside subsidy. They cite two other banking schemes in Indonesia, supervised by the national banking system, as examples of more financially sustainable approaches (see note 3 above).

13. Typical of this new emphasis was the bill passed by Congress in 1987, to require increases in the amounts the U.S. Agency for International Development spends on business investment loans to the poorest of the poor—$50 million in 1988 and $75 million in 1989. The bill gave much greater emphasis to supporting microenterprise among the people at the bottom of the economic ladder.

14. Judith Tendler identified several reasons for the change in the developing nations. She pointed out that the economic conservatism of economists and policy advisors, with its emphasis on "getting prices right," was sympathetic to policy reforms favoring the poorer microentrepreneurs. The fact that financially strapped Third World countries were protecting their own producers from outside competitors was also making it possible for small producers to flourish. A new emphasis on decentralization was creating a more enabling environment for local-level experimentation in the public sector. And public-sector actors, humbled by the disappointing experience of state-sponsored poverty-alleviating initiatives of the 1970s, were becoming more receptive to modest approaches, and learning from the experience of nongovernmental organizations (Tendler, op. cit., pp. iv–vii).

15. The Bangladesh government benefits in the following way: (1) Grameen Bank borrows funds from international banks; (2) loans entering the country arrive in the form of foreign exchange; (3) the government keeps the foreign exchange and transfers the loan equivalent to the bank in Bangladeshi takas; (4) then, when the bank pays interest to international creditors, the government takes a percentage of that interest.

16. Factors that led to famine in Rangpur in 1974 include inefficiencies in governmental economic planning in the years following the country's liberation from Pakistan in 1971; a severe food shortfall in 1972; rapidly rising inflation in 1973; a 63 percent price increase for rice from November 1973 to March 1974; damages sustained from a severe cyclone in late 1973; and a move by the Deputy Commissioner of Rangpur in the early months of 1974 to cancel the allotment of wheat for local relief efforts—just when affordable food sources were diminishing (Alamgir, op. cit., pp. 118–128).

17. Although Yunus and his colleagues were determined to wear just one "hat"— that of the banker—they had certainly not abandoned the idea of using the bank to promote social change. Studies were constantly undertaken to chart the impact of bank efforts. Bank activities appeared to be loosening age-old social restrictions that inhibited economic growth in the countryside. Restrictions on female enterprise were easing and male labor was experiencing improved working conditions. Men, traditionally employed on farms at substandard wages, increasingly received better pay offers from employers. These were trends bank workers encouraged. Employers realized that, without improved wage offers, landless laborers might be able to earn a living by taking out Grameen Bank loans and expanding their off-farm business activities. In some cases the influence of village headmen as judges in village courts declined as Grameen Bank members began to settle disputes among themselves. In short, the

bank encouraged the poor to strengthen their position vis-à-vis more powerful groups by organizing and self-help (Atiur Rahman, "Impact of Grameen Bank Intervention on the Rural Power Structure" [Dhaka: Bangladesh Institute of Development Studies, July 1986]). Bank workers also reported that rising self-respect among borrowers led to reductions in the social frictions of village life. At Chilmari, wife beating had declined. "A husband who beats his wife," explained M. S. Musa, "will find his wife's borrowing group knocking at the door demanding explanation. Often the embarrassed husband stops the abuse, and in a very short time." The burdensome dowry families had to pay the families of their future sons-in-law was also waived in some cases; Grameen Bank workers were encouraging villagers to understand that all could benefit by agreeing to drop the practice.

18. The bank's own move into "joint venture" borrowing arrangements suggests that they themselves realized the importance of larger-scale operations. In such joint ventures, all members of a thirty-person Centre can take out an individual loan, pool the resources, and set up collective enterprises. In Tangail, for instance, one such Centre purchased a shallow tubewell and reached agreement with area farmers to—for a fee—irrigate their lands during the dry season. Initally, the joint-venture concept was popular, and the percentage of lending for such enterprises jumped from 1.9 percent of total bank loans in 1983 to 8.2 percent in 1984. But due to lack of managerial competence and lack of initiative to invest in more advanced forms of production technology, the share fell to 5.1 percent in 1985. A study in 1986 explained, "It is clear . . . that the failure of 'collective enterprises' to expand as fast as 'individual enterprises' is mainly due to slack demand for such loans to undertake non-farm activities or to finance investment on improved technology. Thus, the basic purpose of introducing 'collective enterprise' loans (reaping economies of scale or increasing labour productivity) seems to have been defeated. According to the Grameen Bank management about one-fifth of the collective enterprises undertaken in the initial years failed and they attribute it to the difficulties of maintaining accounts, distrust among members and improper planning about the requirement of working capital for fuller utilisation of machines, etc." (Mahabub Hossain, "Credit for Alleviation of Rural Poverty: The Experience of Grameen Bank in Bangladesh" [Dhaka: Bangladesh Institute of Development Studies, 1986], p. 28).

19. An observation by economist Albert O. Hirschman on the motivation of unorthodox development planners—written about grassroots development in Latin America—might also have relevance for other regions: "The whole venture of grassroots development has arisen in good measure from a revulsion against the worship of the 'gross national product' and of the 'rate of growth' as unique arbiters of economic and human progress. Grassroots development refuses to be judged by these standards. The workers in this vineyard look at their activity as valuable in itself without regard to its 'overall' impact and they do quite well without being reassured at every step by optimistic reports on the macroeconomic consequences of their work. With respect to political effects, participants in grassroots development are similarly convinced that there is something illusory about the importance widely attributed to the largescale political changes—the swinging of the pendulum from autocratic authoritarianism to more or less democratic forms and back again—that have been characteristic of so many countries for so long in Latin America. They are convinced that for political conditions to change more fundamentally, a great many social, cultural and even personal relationships must become transformed" (Albert O. Hirschman, *Getting Ahead Collectively: Grassroots Experiences in Latin America* [New York: Pergamon Press, 1984], pp. 95–96).

6

When the Top Is Not Cooperating: Organizing to Make It against All Odds

SANTA CRUZ, BOLIVIA

In the tropical lowlands of eastern Bolivia, small-scale rice growers were struggling for economic survival. As inflation soared—at times to 23,000 percent—and the national government shifted between military and civilian rule, rural communities could not look to government or banks for even the most basic financial stability. Household savings were in constant jeopardy. In Santa Cruz farmers joined to form a local organization, enlisted the help of a former priest and international aid agencies, carved out for themselves a niche in the region's economy, and managed to get the support of previously opposed local politicians.

He was said to have come to Bolivia in the early 1970s on assignment as a Maryknoll priest. I found him in his backyard picking peas with three of his six children, hands covered with soil. He wore a dirty pair of work pants, a short-sleeve knit shirt not quite large enough to engirdle his bulging middle, and a baseball-style cap with the insignia of San Francisco's pro football team, the 49ers. "Don't mind us," he said, grasping my clean right hand in his. "We're just bringing in a little grub for the table. I'm Dudley Conneely." A parrot perched on a nearby tree echoed "Hello, I'm Dudley, I'm Dudley." Conneely himself grinned. "Our parrot's got even more Irish in 'er than me."

Stories about Dudley Conneely's arrival in Bolivia were, in fact, true. He had come as a young parish priest and settled in the eastern lowland province of Santa Cruz, one of the fastest-growing agricultural regions in the country. But the course of his sojourn had not gone as planned. After several years of running a small church, he wanted to do more about the misery he saw people suffering all around him. The jungles of Santa Cruz had first been opened for clearing and colonization after the 1952 revolution, and again in the 1970s. Increasing the production of sugar and other export crops seemed to Bolivia's military regimes a way to generate needed revenues. With the help and encouragement of U.S. foreign aid, money was invested, roads were built, forests were cleared. Most bank credit went to large-scale sugar plantations, whose operations rapidly grew into a lucrative export trade. But the vast majority of settlers were peasant farmers of indigenous ethnic backgrounds who had come to Santa Cruz from the impoverished highlands hoping for a new start. For them, the outcome had not been so happy. While they did get land, they did not get the loans and farm inputs to make it grow. Seeing their stagnation, Dudley Conneely turned advocate for the *campesinos*, the smallholders, helping them to pool resources, organize, and make their farms operational. His marriage to a local woman of native Andean background, along with the arrival of children and adopted children, sealed his exit from the priesthood in 1978.[1]

"Come inside the house," he said. "I've got visitors and some new gadgets you should see." He led the way into the back of his single-story ranch house, through the kitchen and into a living room, as three small children trailed behind. Some members of the farmers' organization were watching a television set. "Our new VCR," said Dudley. "I filmed their fiesta last week and people are getting their first look at the wonders of video technology. But there's more. Here, let me show you the latest." He pulled the cassette out of the VCR and pushed in another. On came the sounds of a cheering American football crowd, as 49ers quarterback Joe Montana took the snap from center, faded back, and fired a long pass to wide receiver Jerry Rice. Dudley pushed his 49ers cap to the back of his head. "We did pretty well last year," he said with a smile. "My brother in San Francisco sends me all the tapes, and the farmers are getting interested. They don't care at all that these are last year's games." Mrs. Conneely walked into the room with a certain bemused disgust. "I knew we wouldn't be able to keep him away from this toy," she said. "Dudley, don't forget why your guest has come—it's not to see these games." The grin returned to Conneely's face. "Bolivian women, when they get up their Irish, can really be fearsome. OK, before I get myself into deeper trouble, let's get out to the countryside. You should see what the people have done."

At least the reports of what had been done were impressive. Since the mid-1970s a cooperative organization had taken form. Known as the Central de Cooperativas Agropecuarias Mineros, or CCAM, its headquarters were located in Mineros, a small town in northern Santa Cruz. CCAM comprised not only the central organization in Mineros but fifteen community-based cooperatives representing some three hundred partners, or *socios*. Most socios earned a living growing rice, though some had expanded into sugar and vegetables.[2] The cooperative had acquired several trucks, tractors, a bulldozer, and some road-grading vehicles to be rented by members. Its crowning achievement was a mill for processing and storing rice, which freed the socios from having to sell their produce to outside merchants or accept any un-favorable bid offered in the wider rice market at any particular time. Now they could sell their rice for a guaranteed good price to the coop mill, and the mill could store it until the price was good on the national market. The new arrangement was a lifesaver during the mid-1980s when soaring inflation and unscrupulous moneylenders were threatening to put small rice farmers out of business, when labor-short sugarcane growers were pressuring them to sell their land and cut cane on the plantations. CCAM's services enabled small farms to resist caving in, and to thrive. Perhaps even more striking was the emergence in the 1970s of a democratically run organization within the coop during a period of military dictatorship.[3]

Historically, efforts to stabilize small farmer operations in the developing world have not always fared well. Local political and economic activities generally depend on cheap labor. "Power elites" can exert formidable resistance to initiatives aimed to help small farmers, as countless aid agencies have discovered—often too late. Even initially successful organizing efforts are eventually undercut, or their benefits sapped, by opposing elites.[4] In Bangladesh I had encountered a tragic, but not atypical, case of elites sinking a well-meaning program to help the rural poor. An international aid agency had launched a program to make tubewells available to the landless poor so they

John Schnell

could pump underground water and sell it to rich farmers in the dry season. But once the wells became profitable, the better-off farmers took control and ended up selling water back to the poor. In Ethiopia, it has been estimated that up to 20 or 30 percent of U.S. disaster aid during the 1985 famine was skimmed off by powerful urban officials before it reached the needy.[5] The problem of cream skimming by elites is no less marked *within* small farmer organizations. Often a small minority corners the leadership posts, and the benefits, to the exclusion of the many. As one economist put it, "Entrenched and better-off leaders, living off [an organization's] spoils, have been the bane of cooperative history—both North and Latin American."[6]

A growing number of development experts in the 1980s realized that local power elites—whether in or outside the community—might be swayed to stop *opposing* the interests of poorer people, and work *for* them. If the power brokers could not be defeated, they could, in some sense, be co-opted. Aid programs and development strategies that were able to win the powerful to their side had a better chance of success in the long term. Dudley Conneely himself was one of the elites whose support had been secured by the farmers' cooperative of Santa Cruz—albeit at his own volunteering. And the prestige and influence of others within the local community also had been co-opted. But why had CCAM's efforts to position itself in the local power structure succeeded, when so many other cooperative organizations in the area had failed?

No one, according to Dudley, could really grasp the odds CCAM had faced without first seeing the huge mill that serviced the sugar plantations outside Mineros. In a moment the former priest had me on the back of his Honda motorcycle, careering down the highway to Mineros. "You're lucky we've got any fuel today," he shouted in a raspy high voice. "Look at this line of trucks coming up ahead." For at least a mile along the roadside, truck after truck had pulled over to the shoulder, waiting long hours in line for fuel that might, or might not, come. "The gas workers are on strike," explained Dudley. "Periodically, the whole economy comes to a halt. It's always like that here. We never know when the gas workers will be on strike, or the teachers, or the miners. They usually have a point. Over the years our government has badly mismanaged the economy, especially its effects on rural people. Only a few years ago, in 1984 and 1985, inflation was sometimes hitting 23,000 percent. They got the inflation down in the mid-80s, but the stability hasn't yet brought much improvement to the rural economy. People have to do something to survive under those circumstances. What little money they earn, what little buying power they have, vanishes overnight."[7]

The road was paved but dusty and hot under the noonday sun. "Any road here that gets through is considered a nice one," he said. The land was flat and treeless, though in the distance toward the east I could make out a line of forest on the horizon. Only a decade before, these flatlands had been virgin jungle, part of the far western reaches of the great Amazon. Colonization had changed all that. Dudley steered a deliberate course through villages of Japanese settlers—Okinawa 1, Okinawa 2, and Okinawa 3. Japanese investors had come into the area to fell timber from the Amazon and ship it back to the home country. Japanese entrepreneurs had also captured the poultry industry in Bolivia, shipping some of the produce back to Japan, aided by the new international airport (also Japanese-built) in the nearby city of Santa Cruz. "It was designed to take Boeing 747s," said Dudley. "With this airport Japanese investors can stage their commerce here, and all over South America. We've also got some other ethnic settlers from abroad—Indian Sikh families, Koreans, Chinese, Mennonites from Germany and Russia. They all came here when the land was opened for colonization. It makes for a strange mix when you have indigenous groups from Bolivia, the Spanish plantation owners, Japanese, Indians, Chinese, and Russians—all with their own communities and restaurants—right out here in the frontier."

Dudley pulled off the main highway onto a small road lined with palm trees. Through the trees I could see smokestacks in the distance. "That's it," he said. "That's the mill the government set up in 1976 to process sugarcane for export." As we approached the mill, we pulled alongside the loading dock where large trucks dumped the stalks of raw cane. "Once they built this mill, the wealthier farmers began consolidating their holdings around it, to be as close as possible. The trouble with all this is that your economy gets so geared to support the large sugar producers that all the little guys who farm rice get ignored. Most of the bank credit was going to the large farmers. Many rice farmers were tempted to shut down, return to being cane cutters, or to driving taxis in Mineros. Those are dreary ways to earn a living—believe me. Cutting cane stalks and loading them into trucks is backbreaking, dirty work. The only alternative for small farmers was to join together and find ways to make rice farming more profitable and secure. They did it by building a mill of their own—for rice. Its operations are far less extensive than this sugar mill—but, in many ways, far more impressive. They got it going without all the advantages the big guys had."

■

CCAM had set up its headquarters in some small one-story buildings surrounding a courtyard in the nearby town of Mineros. The offices did not look particularly impressive. In the front office a secretary typed on an old Smith-Corona. Along the courtyard, a number of barely furnished rooms had been designated for officers. A few small conference rooms were furnished only with hard wooden chairs and lit by the light of day. But outside were the more visible fruits of the organization's efforts—trucks, trailers, tractors, threshers, road graders, and farm implements, made available at low cost for the use of members. While their number was not nearly enough to go around, what *was* available made a huge difference. Other services included loans, which farmers were allowed to pay back in cash or in rice. Educational programs enabled coop officers to visit major urban centers like Cochabamba or La Paz for training in accounting, organizational management, and other skills needed to run the cooperative. In view of the services it offered, CCAM's headquarters began to look more impressive.

Many Bolivian cooperatives were built on the principles of Rochdale cooperativism in Britain, whose leaders were elected by the membership, rotated in office, and received no pay for performing coop duties. These principles were designed to promote democratic participation and counter the tendency of a privileged few to hog benefits. CCAM, though originally built in the 1970s on the same principles, began by the early 1980s to show patterns of elite domination, contrary to the Rochdale ideal. This deviation intrigued economist Judith Tendler when she visited CCAM at that time. She observed that CCAM's leaders tended to be more prosperous members of the community. The same few were reelected each year and took pay for their services in office. These leaders grew not just rice but also cane. They comprised only 12 percent of the membership, in contrast with the poorer socios who cultivated upland rice. Although the relative prosperity of the "elites" within CCAM actually signified modest means—only a half dozen acres, trivial compared to the plantations of the elites in the outside community—the advantages acquired by CCAM's leaders would have concerned any devotee of Rochdale rules.

But Tendler reasoned that the concentration of leadership among the better-off few can sometimes strengthen a group like CCAM. The interests of leaders can sometimes converge with those of the majority. In CCAM's case both the leaders and the rank-and-file socios had the same desire for higher crop prices, lower transport costs, access to production credit, and lower-cost farm inputs. This convergence contrasted with many other instances of merchants and traders trying to organize coops in larger rural towns.[8] And most of CCAM's elites, Tendler observed, garnered their rewards not by bleeding CCAM's resources but by earning the respect of the community.[9] Yet some years had now passed since Tendler reached those conclusions in 1983. In the meantime some new problems of entrenched leaders had arisen. I wanted to hear from socios themselves how the organization had survived, particularly leaders known for helping the majority.

Dudley led the way across the courtyard toward a conference room where he had asked several socios to meet. As we approached the door, a pickup truck drove in and parked. Three bearded men in green folk outfits got out, looking like a troop of dancers come to entertain. "They're the Russian Mennonites," said Dudley. "Don't let the outfits fool you: This is not dress clothing—it's what they work in. They're some of the hardest workers in the whole of Santa Cruz. And they can drive a hard bargain. They come to make deals with the cooperative for supplies." Inside the conference room were two socios—Jorge and Susano. The dinge of their simple clothes contrasted with the flair of their Russian neighbors' dress, but perhaps typified the work ethic that got CCAM where it was.

Susano Terceros was the upcoming young leader who first became active when, in the late '70s, he moved from the highlands with his family. Like other socios serving as officers, he had gone to the upland town of Cochabamba, and later to the capital, La Paz, to take courses in cooperative organization. Jorge Vallejos was the veteran. He had brought his family to Mineros from the upland town of Sucre in 1969. With the help of the cooperative, Jorge had succeeded not only in rice production but in corn, sugar, and vegetables. He had served in all the main offices of the cooperative. When Jorge lost an eye in the early '80s, the cooperative issued emergency loans to buy an artificial one. One thing Jorge had not lost was pride that he knew how to make a coop work when others had failed.

■

Jorge: "Other coops fail in Santa Cruz because a few people take the benefits for themselves. Sometimes they get farmers together just to say they have the legal number you need to form a cooperative and qualify for bank loans.[10] We decided not to work that way. We made

Susano Terceros (left), Jorge Vallejos (right)

a rule not to allow anyone to be president more than one year, or to stay in other offices more than three years in a row. And we keep all our trucks available to everyone. Even farmers who don't belong to CCAM can rent our trucks or take out loans."

Susano: "The rice mill is a big reason why benefits get spread around. In the beginning, everyone realized that the equipment was getting used more by the leaders. Some wanted to expand into sugar. But deciding to build a rice mill was what the majority wanted. That would allow us to give better prices to all the socios. Now they can be sure their rice is weighed honestly. Before this, people could get deceived by middlemen and merchants."

Jorge: "Even with those features, the organization has also needed a lot of watching. We set up a Vigilance Committee to keep an eye on it. And by hiring Carlos—he's a trained accountant—we're finally able to keep stricter control of the books. His training had made a big difference for keeping things fair."

Susano: "Yes, we had troubles with some leaders. I remember when Florentino was president in 1980. He began selling our rice to friends outside the coop at prices that were lower than market prices. He gave back to CCAM the amount it was due, but this hurt us in the end, for word got out that CCAM rice was being sold at lower prices than our coop price. That is why a Vigilance Committee was needed to watch over the officers."

Jorge: "With that—and Carlos watching over the books—I think our problems with the leaders were over."

Susano: "But one way our leaders have helped CCAM is their connections with other organizations. This made other organizations take us seriously. Some cooperatives do not get that kind of support. Jorge himself is a member of the Federation of Cane Growers in Santa Cruz, and a friend of the president. He got the Federation to support us when we asked for a quota to sell our sugar to the sugar mill. This adds to what we can earn from our rice."

Jorge: "Another member is on the board of the sugar mill. Once we got the sugar people to recognize us, that ended a lot of hostility that existed before. We began to be recognized in the local economy. We were no longer having to struggle with rich people all the time just to survive."[11]

■

If CCAM derived strength from socios who had local and regional clout, not all observers of the coop agreed that benefits for the majority truly outweighed those for the better-off minority. Anthropologist Leslie Gill argued that the leaders benefited disproportionately from the cooperative's loan program, tractors, mechanical shop, and consumer store—especially in the early days when they wanted to expand into sugar. Moreover, she contended, the coop enabled elites to "forge new ties among themselves and establish links to other social groups and institutions."[12] Other observers, including some of CCAM's funders, warned that the coop was not doing enough to educate the rank and file in leadership skills, endangering organizational survival in the longer run.[13]

But observers like Judith Tendler cautioned about expecting too much democracy out of a cooperative in the Bolivian context. There, she proposed, the strength of leadership provided by the better-off members was a critical element in competing and negotiating with external forces, and so more than justified itself in the eyes of members. "It is *we* who are disappointed . . . [and who] live in dread fear that [coops] will turn out, under close scrutiny, to be dominated by elites. . . . [I]t is important to see the difficulty of the fit between our hopeful vision of the coops and the historical experience from which they are copied [as in Santa Cruz]."[14]

When it came to another set of players—CCAM's international donors—coop observers were in general agreement. The donors played a decisive role in helping the coop to stabilize its position in the Santa Cruz economy. Start-up funding came from international development organizations, amounting to well over a million dollars in loans and grants from 1974 to 1982. The greatest support came from the Inter-American Foundation (IAF), (West Germany's) Bread for the World, the Inter-American Development Bank, and the Canadian International Development Agency.[15] This availability of cash and loans was explained in no small part by the rural development priority that emerged worldwide in the 1970s.

I had timed my visit to coincide with the arrival in Mineros of one foundation's representative—the Inter-American Foundation's Kevin Healy. A Cornell-trained sociologist in his early forties, Healy was one of the new-style philanthropists who traipsed off into the rural areas of the developing world in the 1970s. He got started in the late '60s with a stint in Peru in the Peace Corps. During the '70s and '80s, Healy had come to be a kind of one-man bank, traveling the country top to bottom year after year, seeking out grassroots ventures that could benefit from small grants or loans. "The foundation was set up by an act of Congress," he explained, as we sat over breakfast in Dudley Conneely's kitchen. "Some people assume this was done as part of the Democratic Party's agenda to help the poor in the 1970s. But the origins really go back to 1968 and the new Republican administration. Dissatisfaction had been growing over the Alliance for Progress begun by President Kennedy. Investments in large-scale development projects—though they benefited people who were already better off—were not having the intended effect in reducing poverty among the majority. Republicans said, 'We're tired of working through government bureaucracies—too much red tape, and the money gets siphoned off.' The new idea was to scale down our assistance programs, have more modest goals, target efforts more toward the grassroots, and ensure that the assistance we gave had tangible benefits for the poor. The legislation establishing the Inter-American Foundation passed in 1969, though we did not become operational until 1971."

In the '70s, the IAF developed a reputation across Latin America for being detached from political or military interests of the U.S. government. During the Reagan years, it had proved no easy task to maintain this reputation. U.S. foreign aid, including humanitarian aid, was generally oriented *away* from economic development toward political and military goals, the most prominent being the anticommunist causes of Central America.[16] The IAF came under some suspicion in 1983 when its Reagan-appointed board fired the IAF president and later replaced him with a wealthy benefactress of the Republican Party with little professional experience in Latin American affairs. She owned several deluxe health clubs, and so was dubbed the "Spa Queen." Still, across the many Latin American countries where it had worked, the IAF managed to keep its reputation remarkably unsoiled, even in the most hotly political contexts.

Healy had come to Bolivia as much an outsider as any other visiting North American. But over the years he had become, to a remarkable degree, "one of the people." For reasons he himself wasn't sure of, he had acquired the nickname "Benito." Whenever he arrived in Bolivia, twice a year, word spread across the Andean peaks and the Amazonian lowlands that Benito was back. And so, to the people, he must have seemed something like the hero of television's "Millionaire," searching out the needy and dispensing grants in the name of some distant unseen source. But perhaps a more precise characterization of Healy, and of others like him, came from the economist Albert Hirschman. While touring Latin American coops in the mid-1980s, Hirschman was struck by the myriad of local service organizations that had emerged in the '70s and '80s, largely due to the assistance of volunteers and younger-generation idealists from other countries, working for international aid groups. These idealists were not prepared to wait for government policies to change before the vast array of popular needs could be met. Latin American governments have rarely provided the services, training, or economic incentives that rural communities need. International agencies like the

Kevin Healy

IAF, along with young professionals from all walks of life, tried to fill the vacuum and help local organizations stand on their own feet. As Hirschman put it, "While it is . . . true that the Inter-American Foundation and other grassroots funding agencies often work closely with [local organizations] to make contact with the 'real' grassroots, the men and women of these [funding agencies] do not at all think of themselves as having 'set up in business' to serve as intermediaries between international donors and grassroots recipients. All of these entities were established in response to pressing social, political, and economic problems . . . and out of the new perception . . . that it was possible to do something about these problems at the local level regardless of whatever large-scale 'structural' changes were needed or likely to happen at the national level."[17]

By the late '80s the IAF's financial contribution to CCAM had slowed. But this trend, in Healy's view, was testimony to the success of support given in the past. "The significant thing is that the cooperative has now graduated from us and can deal with larger financial institutions. We helped them to get their feet on the ground, and to get the rice mill going. But now they're taking out much larger loans from local banks, from the Inter-American Development Bank, and others.[18] The rice mill also helped to get their voice heard by politicians in La Paz. At one point when the government was planning to import rice from abroad, CCAM stepped in and protested. To the government's credit, they listened. Ten years ago that never would have happened."

■

The rice mill was the most visible trophy of CCAM. To see it, Dudley Conneely insisted at the end of breakfast, was to know the real soul of what had been achieved. "It's come to represent for people all across the district what can be done when people put their mind to something." The mill was situated on the edge of jungle on the main road leading out of Mineros. In its own way, the mill's layout paralleled that of the sugar mill, only on a much smaller scale. A building near the entry gate served as a receiving station, with equipment for weighing trucks and loads of incoming rice. Across the courtyard, a large warehouse housed the rice-milling machines. Nearby stood a cluster of 30-foot aluminum storage silos. The thirty-person full-time staff paled by comparison with the hundreds employed by the sugar mill, but was impressive by local campesino standards.

"What all this really means," said Dudley, "is that socios can now control their own destiny in ways they never could before. They not only process the rice they grow; they can also hold it in storage and sell it when market prices are high. Before, they had no control. Just had to unload it at harvest to whoever would buy, whether a middleman, trader, or one of the other small millers nearby. The prices they got were terrible. Now they can sell at competitive prices. They're assured of getting their rice weighed correctly. Their competitiveness also has a ripple effect in the wider economy, making the system fairer and freer. And, you know, the mill saved farms during the years of hyperinflation—not one farm failed during that period, even though some farmers' income dropped in half."

Outside, workers in bare feet shoveled piles of raw rice into wheelbarrows, to take inside for processing. Others piled up white bags of fully processed rice ready for market. Inside, the atmosphere was charged with the hum of rice mills, drying machines, and conveyor belts. Sophistication in processing had reached the level of producing four grades of rice—fine, semifine, rough, and raw. Dudley led the way out of the warehouse to the silos, climbed the aluminum rungs to a square hole in the silo wall, and popped his 49ers cap inside, as if to say, Yes, it's real. "You know," he said, jumping down, "when you support ventures like this, you can wonder if the people may be getting too dependent on you. But in the end, really, I just got them going. When they went to the bank it helped for them to have the Padre along—with me there, it was tougher for the bankers to refuse. But once the farmers' organization and the mill got going, the campesinos realized they were able to stand for themselves. The irony is, as an outsider trying to help, you only know you've really succeeded if, in the end, you've phased yourself out."[19]

1. The origins of colonization in Santa Cruz go back to broader Bolivian land reforms after the revolution of 1952. A new coalition government took power promising better conditions for the country's peasant majority, and land redistribution was begun. Another redistribution program followed in the 1971 to 1978 period under the military regime of Hugo Banzer. Some six million hectares were affected—on top of the nine million repartitioned during the 1950s. In the province of Obispo Santisteban (where Dudley Conneely settled), the vast majority of beneficiaries of the 1971–78 reform were property owners with less than fifty hectares, but they controlled only 11 percent of the land. Individuals who owned properties over 500 hectares represented 10 percent of the total beneficiaries but controlled 83 percent of the land. The outcome was consistent with Banzer's policy to substitute national production for reliance on imports and also increase surpluses for export. Large farms were believed to have greater productive potential than small ones. Availability of national bank credit favored rapid cash-crop production of sugar and cotton. During the 1970s, over 68 percent of all commercial credit in the country went to the Santa Cruz area. Peasant settlers and migrant workers supplied the labor needed to sustain agro-industrial growth (Lesley J. Gill, "Commercial Agriculture and Peasant Production: A Case Study of Agrarian Reformism and the Development of Capitalism in Northern Santa Cruz, Bolivia" [Ann Arbor, MI: University Microfilms International, 1984], pp. 45–88).

2. Rice was popular among colonists not only for making subsistence possible, but because varieties common to the area were relatively easy to cultivate, requiring little capital or soil preparation, and because the harvest could be easily stored and marketed.

3. The Santa Cruz area saw widespread experimentation with organizing after the 1952 revolution. Early peasant organizing took the form of *sindicatos*—local-level political organizations, usually with fewer than 200 members. According to Herbert S. Klein, much of the strength of peasant organization well into the '70s and '80s was rooted in the sindicatos experience (H. S. Klein, *Bolivia: The Evolution of a Multi-*

Ethnic Society [New York & Oxford: Oxford University Press, 1982], p. 234]. Just after the revolution, sindicatos were set up to receive arms and create local militias. But the sindicatos also asserted land claims for members, even in the absence of formal legal title, did infrastructure building, and defended other rights that had been gained in the revolution (Gill, op. cit., p. 137). During the regime of Hugo Banzer in 1971–78, policy makers attempted to increase their political hold and promote the growth of modern commercial economy by "depoliticizing" and "reeducating" the peasant masses along more submissive lines (Klein, op. cit., p. 255). In this climate sindicatos could not be tolerated and were largely repressed, while cooperatives—organized on more strictly economic lines—were allowed, and became the focus of peasant organizing efforts. Originally legalized in 1958, these organizations were permitted to produce raw materials and perform processing, marketing, and consumer services. In practice they also began to provide more and more advocacy for small farmers, especially to help ensure that their lands were not subsumed by large plantations (Gill, op. cit. p. 151).

4. Judith Tendler, "Rural Projects through Urban Eyes: An Interpretation of the World Bank's New-style Rural Development Projects," World Bank Staff Working Paper No. 532 (Washington, DC: World Bank, 1982).

5. David K. Willis, "Ethiopia Makes Money on Donated Food Aid," *The Christian Science Monitor,* May 26, 1985.

6. Judith Tendler, *What to Think about Cooperatives: A Guide from Bolivia* (Washington, DC: The Inter-American Foundation, 1983), Overview, p. 24. She wrote, "Those who criticize the choice of cooperatives as instruments of development argue that, when successful, these organizations tend to become self-serving 'capitalist' enterprises that benefit a small elite membership, and often end up exploiting the poorer members of the community. A frequently cited example of such selfishness is the way production coops treat their seasonal labor: as soon as these coops start to do well, they close their ranks and shift their work obligations to outside, low-paid laborers, whom they will not allow to join the coop, let alone to unionize."

7. Changes in Bolivia's national economic policies in the mid-1980s brought rampant inflation under control and introduced some financial stability to the Bolivian economy. But by the late '80s even those involved in redesigning those strategies, such as Harvard economist Jeffrey Sachs, were increasingly concerned that economic stabilization had not yet translated into widespread developmental benefits for the broader population (Jeffrey D. Sachs, *Developing Country Debt and the World Economy* [Chicago and London: University of Chicago Press, 1989], pp. 78–79; see all of this chapter on the forces that created Bolivia's economic crisis).

8. Tendler, op. cit., Overview, p. 25. Judith Tendler observed that the CCAM leaders initially put priority on acquiring the equipment needed to clear stumps from land, enabling them to shift into sugar production. But their next move benefited CCAM's rank-and-file rice growers. While rice production was not the highest priority of the better-off leaders, they opted next to concentrate efforts on the rice mill (Tendler, op. cit., p. 239). Tendler further identified some "structural factors" in CCAM's environment that drew the association into a successful rice-milling operation with strong equalizing effects throughout the membership: (1) the impracticality of going into cane milling, (2) the widespread cultivation in Santa Cruz of a crop (rice) for which the processing task was relatively easy, (3) the centrality of this crop to poorer members' income, in addition to its being cultivated by the better-off cane growers, and (4) the fact that agroprocessing was an easier task than that of the credit, transport, and equipment operations taken on by CCAM (Tendler, op. cit., Overview, p. 31).

9. Tendler wrote, "In many Latin American communities, a community leader is expected to perform at least some socially responsible deeds. The coop provides an opportunity for the leader to meet these expectations, as a way of achieving and maintaining status in his community. By drawing on entrenched community leaders, then, the coop can be seen as hitching certain socially obligated persons to its cause" (Tendler, op. cit., Overview, p. 35). Lesley Gill depicted the situation of one CCAM official, Don Ignacio Betanzos, who was president for five years in the early period: "The better-off members sought individual gain from a project intended to benefit the entire cooperative, but by supporting collective maintenance, Don Ignacio was able to further his own economic interests and appear as a defender of the poor. He not only maintained partial control over the care and use of the cattle at a time when he was unprepared to buy his own, but also strengthened his position as a leader in the eyes of the . . . socios" (Gill, op. cit., p. 251).

10. Agrarian reform legislation allowed for acquisition of lands by cooperatives. These operations were supposed to function, in theory, as collectively owned production units. In practice, however, such groups contained entrepreneurs who hired wage laborers and called themselves a cooperative in order to expedite the long process of acquiring legal title to unclaimed lands (Kevin Healy, "Power, Class, and Rural Development in Southern Bolivia" [Ithaca, NY: Cornell University, 1979] Ph.D. thesis).

11. Jorge was one of the better-off farmers who was able to grow both rice and sugar. He had invested profits from rice and potatoes into expanding his sugar plantings. The advantage of growing sugar over rice lies in the fact that cane stalks can be cut without destroying their root systems, allowing for new growth without replanting. CCAM gave loans and transport vehicles to such better-off farmers. CCAM also purchased shares in the association of large sugar growers and the sugar mill (UNAGRO), qualifying CCAM members to sell their sugar produce to the mill up to a certain quota.

12. Gill, op. cit., pp. 161–162. She further wrote about the better-off coop leaders, "Their common interests as cane producers may temporarily align them with the [wealthy owners of capital-intensive farming]. This occurred in October, 1981, after the sugar mills delayed payments, and rumors of devaluation created alarm among producers who feared that their eventual incomes would be drastically reduced. By way of response, the Federacion de Caneros, with the support of the Federacion Departamental de Caneros Campesinos y Productores Agricolas and the Federacion de Caneros de Colonias, ordered sugar cane shipments to the mills halted and blockaded roads in northern Santa Cruz. Growers hoped not only to pressure both state and privately owned mills into paying them but also demanded that payments be adjusted to the new exchange rate in case of a devaluation. CCAM sugar growers enthusiastically backed the strike and suspended shipments to the mills. They did not resume them until the president of the Federacion de Caneros officially called off the strike. Despite their common interests as sugar cane producers, the small cane growers of CCAM cannot always be counted on to support the [wealthier owners of capital-intensive farms]. Pressured by more efficient capitalist producers and oppressed by state policies which support the agroindustries, they may join with other groups to support broad-based populist concerns" (Gill, op. cit., pp. 255–256). Lesley Gill did not deny, however, that considerable benefits accrued to worse-off socios, in the form of better prices from the rice mill, transport facilities, and jobs in the mill (p. 227). And she recognized that entrenched leaders can also enhance the organization's continuity as a service and income-earning enterprise. They often bring with them considerable entrepreneurial experience and drive that make the difference between success

and failure of business ventures. Moreover, they can give force to the group's negotiation with outside groups (p. 238).

13. Interview, October 1989, with Kevin Healy, Inter-American Foundation, in Washington, DC. Hirschman also noted, however, that often the normal expectations about education—requiring education first, then organizational and social progress second—could, in fact, work the other way around. "We have been strongly conditioned to think that education is a prime mover and a precondition to development . . . the sequence can be the other way round, that education (training in literacy, arithmetic, etc.) will often be *induced* by development" (Albert O. Hirschman, *Getting Ahead Collectively: Grassroots Experiences in Latin America* [New York: Pergamon Press, 1984], p. 9).

14. Tendler, op. cit., p. 258. Tendler cited the story of one CCAM elite, Don Ignacio Betanzos: "Don Ignacio's educational background gave him the necessary skills to undertake the administrative tasks of the cooperative, and his varied experience in Santa Cruz had brought him into contact with a cross section of people from culturally distinct backgrounds. His abilities to speak Quechua, a skill learned from the workers of his family's property, as well as to adopt a lowland Spanish accent enabled him to accumulate a multi-ethnic following. He rapidly advanced from treasurer to president of the Central" (op. cit., Overview, p. 35).

15. From Bread for the World, over $600,000; from the Inter-American Development Bank, $500,000 in credit loans; from the Canadian International Development Agency, a loan for a lathe; and from the Inter-American Foundation, over $150,000 for the rice silos, consumer store, emergency fund, and other items. In addition, some tractors and trucks were secured through a donation from Caterpillar Company in Illinois.

16. The sensitivity about U.S. aid to the region has partly to do with the extensive involvement of American aid in the post-revolution period, as well as the linkages of that aid to U.S. foreign policy. Bolivia was the first Latin American nation to receive food aid through the U.S. Food for Peace Program in 1953, partly in conjunction with agreements to acquire minerals from Bolivia and partly with American efforts to counteract communist influence in the region. Herbert S. Klein wrote, "By the end of the decade of massive aid Bolivia had achieved the extraordinary distinction of having obtained $100 million dollars in United States aid, making it at the time the largest single recipient of United States aid in Latin America and the highest per capita in the world. So dependent upon this aid did Bolivia become that, by 1958, one-third of its budget was paid for directly by United States funds" (Klein, op. cit., p. 238). Between 1976 and 1979, the U.S. Agency for International Development (AID) poured $132.1 million into agricultural projects in the Santa Cruz area (Gill, op. cit., p. 223, citing statistics from the La Paz office of AID).

17. Hirschman, op. cit., p. 79. He also wrote: "One of the most characteristic features of the current social scene in Latin America is the ubiquitous presence of so-called 'intermediate' organizations that have taken it upon themselves to do 'social promotion' [*promocion social*] among the poorer sections in the cities of the countryside. Formed typically by young professionals—lawyers, economists, sociologists, social workers, architects, agronomists, priests, or former priests, etc.—these organizations often attempt to combine research and action. But their principal motivation is to 'go to the people' and help them" (pp. 6–7).

18. In 1982 CCAM negotiated its first loan with the Inter-American Development Bank (IDB), as part of a larger grant assistance package from IDB. The long-term loan was intended to set up a rotating credit fund for CCAM members. In 1986 a second

agreement was reached, with IDB financing $300,000 in loans and $73,000 in technical assistance ("Central de Cooperativas Agropecuarias Mineros," Inter-American Foundation paper prepared for in-house evaluation in 1988, unpublished, pp. 8–9).

19. Judith Tendler wrote, "The outside advisors of the Bolivian groups functioned not only in a technical capacity but also as powerful patrons. They brokered for the coop with state agencies and other donors, playing a crucial role in gaining access to other resources and to favorable government decisions on regulatory and tax matters. In the case of CCAM, the brokering was probably even more important to the federation's growth than any management skills that were imparted by its patron priest. . . . Resentment to CCAM's patron-priest also was low, probably because his power as a broker was much greater than that of the other two outsiders: he arranged for all CCAM's outside grants, managed the acquisition of most of their equipment and spare parts (much of it, for free), negotiated tariff exemptions for equipment imports, and arranged for the credit they received from the local banking system. At the same time, his lack of experience in management and accounting, and his role as a promoter rather than a technician, did not give him the formal authority or the taste to get as deeply involved in everyday management matters as a professional manager or accountant would have" (Tendler, op. cit., pp. 203–205).

PART THREE

Energies in the Learning Process

7

When Economy and Nature Get in Sync: Easing Man-Nature Warfare in the Himalayas

SUKHOMAJRI, INDIA

Villagers in the Himalayan foothills of northern India were caught in a downward spiral of poverty and environmental destruction. The classic dilemma seemed inescapable: Survive now by cutting trees and grazing animals across the eroded hills, but do so at the cost of destroying natural resources on which future generations will depend. The government's conservation demands had been ignored by villagers, and quick-fix technological solutions were going nowhere, when a new approach was tried. Combining the ideas of development workers and villagers themselves, the plan rapidly began to reverse land destruction, regenerate the hills, and bring a surge of prosperity surpassing all expectations. But early gains were short-lived. Only when plans were refined to become part of a broader learning process in village life did more lasting answers emerge—a model singled out by national leaders for replication across the entire region.

At 4 A.M. the highway leading north out of Delhi was treacherous. Fog intensified the predawn dark. My driver, Rajiv, seemed sufficiently adept at negotiating the misty curves, braving the threat of oncoming headlights to pass truck after truck laden with goods for market. Never mind the lack of visibility. Never mind the tight passing margin on the narrow two-laned road, or the vulnerability of bicyclists trying to share the asphalt. For Rajiv, these were matters of

course. And he took seriously, too seriously, the task of reaching
Sukhomajri without delay.

Mercifully, sunrise rolled back the fog, and automobile travel became a more reasonable proposition. By now bicyclists sported full
beards and colored turbans. We had entered the outskirts of Chandigarh, capital of the Sikh state of Punjab and of the Hindu state of
Haryana. Modern features, from its construction in the 1950s to its
man-made lake, destined Chandigarh to be odd man out among India's more ancient urban centers. The city's Swiss-born architect, le
Corbusier, had wanted it that way. But we had no time to linger over
his urban artifact. Rajiv veered northeast toward the Himalayan foothills of Haryana. "We're not far now from Sukhomajri," he said. The
landscape grew more mountainous and barren, though the rise from
the southern plain was still gradual, the valleys wide, and the roadside interrupted by occasional squatters' huts, a cement factory, fruit
and vegetable stands. It was impossible not to sense the presence of
glaciered peaks to the north. "When the haze lifts out there, you will
see the Himalayas," said Rajiv. Already the cool exhilaration of Hil-
lary's fabled ascent seemed to waft down from Tibetan heights.

I first heard about Sukhomajri from economists returning to the
United States from northwest India. The Americans were convinced
that a certain clear-sightedness had been reached in that small village, something that all too often eludes those who try to help the
rural poor. The annals of foreign aid are full of the tales of inter-
twined social and environmental forces that defy understanding,
deceive the planners, and spoil success. Pull the wrong "string" in
the poverty tangle and, even with the best intentions to free things
up, you tie the knot tighter. This time, it was said, the pitfalls had
been avoided, essential connections revealed. Moreover, the observers talked about Sukhomajri with a kind of delight, a surprised wonder, like the exhilaration evoked by watching a rare event in nature,
or stumbling upon a rare piece of art precisely where no one thought
it could be.

Rajiv turned off the main road and followed a gullied dirt lane
through green fields to the edge of a small settlement. "This is it,"
he said. "Your man is waiting." Rameesh Bansar was a young engineer with the Chandigarh branch of the Central Soil and Water Conservation Research and Training Institute. "Come," he said, wasting
no time to head for the village center. "At first this looks pretty

stereotypical of village life just about anywhere in India," he said, "but don't let that fool you." I promised not to be fooled. In his knit cap and hooded blue jacket, Rameesh looked more the ranger ready for a day on the glaciers than an engineer out for a village stroll on a comfortably cool winter day. But he seemed right about the apparent normalcy of village life in Sukhomajri. Modest family dwellings clustered in no apparent order. Schoolchildren dashed through narrow passageways, while women returned from their daily search for water, balancing weighty, oversized vessels with seeming effortlessness on their heads. Cows and buffalo were tethered in domestic courtyards, the stench of their droppings tingeing the sweetness of country air.

But when we cleared the residential area, village "normalcy" ended abruptly at a gaping gorge that cut through the hills, dropping fifty feet into the earth, at points more, and stretching as far as the eye could see. Erosion had exposed layer upon layer of the sediment with which time had shaped the ancient Shivalik hills. Rock-strewn gullies cut through the canyon walls, converging to the floor below. "A veritable warfare was going on between the people and these hills," explained Rameesh. "It's the pattern all over—villagers grazing their livestock across the hills, cutting down trees for fuel, denuding the hills of the vegetation, exposing soils to torrential monsoon rains. But you don't realize the seriousness of the erosion that results until you see how it can carve out a canyon like this." Each year the precipice was drawing closer and closer to the village itself. Starting in the late 1960s, acre after acre of the village's best farmland began to break away in huge chunks and plunge into the gorge. Rameesh touched his hand to his forehead and pointed across the gulf. "If aerial photographs had been taken, they would have shown a village literally coming to be swallowed up by the gorge."

In fact, Sukhomajri's apocalyptic peril—like so much environmental degradation—had not developed with apocalyptic suddenness. It was the product of a century and a half of continuous deforestation and environmental destruction, wreaking havoc all across the Himalayan foothills from Pakistan on the west to Nepal on the east. Early nineteenth century British accounts of the hills spoke of luxurious forests of oak, silver fir, deodar, and other species. But in the 1830s mining contractors began cutting trees to clear access to iron and copper deposits in the northern hills. More deforestation followed

British efforts to secure military control of the region. After subjugating the Sikh population of Punjab in the 1850s, the British cleared valleys of trees and settled village communities sympathetic to British rule. More forests were leveled to make way for construction of officers' personal vacation retreats, with lavishly manicured lawns. Timber was felled to build the railways that would carry tea and other raw materials to ships at port. Meanwhile nomadic herding people also began to settle in the valleys. They grazed their animals over the surrounding hills and allowed them to eat whatever vegetation remained. By the time India gained independence in 1947, the ground cover that once protected the rich topsoils of the Himalayan foothills had almost totally vanished.[1]

The predicament of an isolated village like Sukhomajri might have gone totally unnoticed except for the community's curious relationship with the residents of le Corbusier's city, Chandigarh, some twenty kilometers to the south. The city's huge showpiece lake was literally filling up with silt washed down from the hills. Sukhomajri just happened to lie at the headwater of the main ravine that carried silt to the lake. By 1970 the lake was nearly half filled. Forestry officials—at the urging of Chandigarh's troubled citizens—coaxed and cajoled the people of Sukhomajri to stop grazing their animals and felling trees. Villagers promised to cooperate. But the grazing went on. Forestry officials threatened legal reprisals. Villagers agreed to cooperate. Grazing went on. To villagers there seemed no alternative, for cattle were their livelihood. And so year after year grazing went on, more of the hills washed away, village poverty approached destitution, and the canyon opened its ugly mouth even wider.[2]

"Fortunately," explained Rameesh, "there was a way to reverse the downward spiral, and it has been happening with astonishing speed. Come." He led the way up a steep path to the top of a hill overlooking the gorge. "As the frustration of forestry officials mounted, the state government finally involved P. R. Mishra, my boss at the Central Soil and Water Conservation Research and Training Institute at Chandigarh. I'll take you to meet him. They thought he'd just build some dams at the headwater, break the water's flow, and slow the erosion. And at first that was done. But Mishra was thinking in much broader terms. He spent time with villagers who actually lived at the headwater. There were many discussions. It's Mishra's way— he's always

asking questions, many questions. There were also discussions with outside experts. In the process, it was discovered that the real problem did not lie in the forest but in village poverty. 'Naked people, naked hills,' he says, 'can you clothe one without clothing the other?' Getting villagers to stop grazing animals and allow the hills to recover meant giving them some real economic alternative, not just threats of jail. That alternative lay in the water trapped in the dams. A bargain was struck: We would arrange for irrigation pipes to be built to get that water to farmers' fields. This would allow farmers to grow extra crops during the dry season. Villagers, in exchange, would have to agree to voluntarily stop grazing their animals across the hills. Mishra calls the arrangement *social fencing.*"[3]

Looking east, I could see three reservoirs perched on the ledge above the gorge, Sukhomajri's fields extending just beyond. "But don't misunderstand," said Rameesh. "The solution here went far beyond a simple bargain—that would miss the beauty of what was taking form.

What you really see at Sukhomajri is a radical adjustment in the way people relate to their environment. I want you to understand this from Mishra himself." From my vantage point looking across the hills, one result of this adjustment was already clear. The hills had regained a substantial new cover of grasses, shrubs, and trees. And not a single grazing animal could be seen feeding on the new plants. I was beginning to sense the significance of Sukhomajri. Where economy and nature had been at odds, the conflict had been ended and the two brought in sync. The way livestock were kept and fed on village grounds was not mere happenstance; the social fence was at work, keeping animals off the hills. "Livestock are now being fed from renewable grasses we planted over the hills," said Rameesh. "The root systems are not destroyed, nor are the bushes and trees." Indeed, land around the village evidenced the greenness of the young wheat and vegetables made possible by irrigation. If anything remained a curiosity, it was the fact that Sukhomajri's prosperity came not by cutting back on village use of hill vegetation, but by *increasing* it.

■

Rameesh agreed to take me to the house of Mishra himself. "At first I thought this fellow a bit mad, with all his notions about the linkages of poverty and ecology," Rameesh said, stepping into a Land-Rover for the drive to Chandigarh. "But then I began to realize that Mishra has an extraordinary grasp of the interrelations of people, their economy, and ecosystem." We arrived at a modest brick dwelling on the outskirts of the city and were met by a man getting on in years. He wore a gray sportcoat and a checkered black-and-white scarf hung loosely around his neck—the sort of scarf frequently carried by men to protect their ears from seasonal cool winds. Rameesh introduced his boss as "Mishra-ji," the honorific showing respect. Though Mishra was a shy man, the squint of his eyes and the purse of his lips seemed to draw an intensity of concentration to the front of his face. "I'm happy to be able to tell you that we're finally putting an end to this warfare between the hills and the people," he said. Sentences spilled out so rapidly, so packed with information, that I feared Mishra's exuberance in communication would overwhelm my ability to comprehend. But Rameesh was right. This was someone with an extraordinary grasp of things human and natural, especially how they interrelate.[4]

"We had to abandon the old approach to conservation," he explained, as his wife served a tray of hot tea. "The old approach of the Forestry Department looked at conservation as a *technical* problem you could solve in isolation from poverty and human need. Villagers were seen as a mechanical link in the technological solution. From this standpoint you just tried to make them stop cutting trees, plant new ones, and then wait twenty or thirty years before they could use the forest again. But this meant a lot of waiting, which poor people can't afford to do.[5] Our new approach treated ecological and economic needs *together*, not separately. To be sure, you need to do reforestation. You plant fast-growing trees and grasses. The Indian sun is powerful, so these plants can grow very, very fast. But you also have a plan by which people can *use* the new vegetation immediately. They can cut the top branches of trees after only a year or two, getting some of the fuel they need while not destroying the trees. Meanwhile, by cutting the grasses above the root they get fodder for their cattle while not destroying the plants. So you see, there are ways to increase the growth of vegetation while at the same time using more of that vegetation. This is what conservation really means: Grow more, and use more of what you grow, in order to conserve more."[6]

Mishra grinned at the reversal of common reason. "When you think about it, the idea of making poor people wait and curb their consumption never really made sense anyway. The energy and growing power of nature are not waiting—not the rainfall, not the sun's energy, not the capacity of the land to support vegetation. So why the people? With a little ingenuity, they can conserve more by producing more. And once you establish this alliance between conservation and economic production, you have no dearth of anything. The people are not waiting, the land is not waiting, nothing waits or is lacking. You see it at Sukhomajri with your own eyes."[7]

■

Sukhomajri's model for hill regeneration had achieved what scientific researchers sometimes call "elegance." Inadequate concepts yield to more adequate ones. Previously unproductive and degenerative combinations *re*combine, with advances in performance of the whole. Sukhomajri seemed to confirm, in one small corner of India, the possibility of realizing the late twentieth century ideal of bringing human economy in line with a regeneration of nature.[8] The elegance of the model was enhanced by its answering the moral dilemma that besets the environmental reform in poor nations—the conflict between the right of poor people to consume natural resources just to survive and the call of the broader society for them to save resources for generations yet unborn. By the late 1980s a growing number of development analysts confirmed that poor people would participate in environmental preservation only if it also gave them a better *livelihood*.[9] Sukhomajri's hill restoration quickly brought economic rewards, reduced the vulnerability to hunger, and so had a chance for permanent support from villagers.[10]

To those working inside the experiment since it began in 1975, what was happening had a fascination verging on the religious. Even the most hard-core scientists seemed somewhat awed at the productive potentials being released. Mishra and his colleagues wondered, at least half seriously, if they had tapped into some little-known cosmic force. The journalistic observer learns to be cautious about such speculation, so rife is the Indian subcontinent with impassioned social reformers claiming inside visions of truth. This time, given the rapid change achieved at Sukhomajri, I was inclined to forgive Mishra and his colleagues if they indulged in a bit of wonder. But it was the pragmatism of change, not the cosmological speculations, that intrigued Western observers. Planners with the experiment had not only discerned "essential connections," but were also willing to learn, to change and refine their strategy as time went on. The importance of the *learning process* in rural development is seldom conveyed by the Western media. But to those involved professionally, process has become nearly as much goal as means. No matter how well a plan seems to be integrated with human and natural realities at the outset, unanticipated social, political, and ecological forces inevitably surface—no less critical to sustaining progress over time. Observation is needed to assess the course of events, and what necessary adjustments the events demand. Organizational behaviorist David Korten dubbed it a "learning process approach."[11]

Broader global concern over "process" first intensified in the late 1970s, with the growing realization that many "well-planned" Western aid projects had failed. A large number of planners had not, for a variety of reasons, taken the learning process seriously. Some were under pressure to get quick results, and did not allow time for process—a not infrequent problem with congressionally mandated aid programs. In other cases, planners went for the technological quick fix and were simply not aware of the importance of process. Whatever the reasons, developing country landscapes have been littered with "white elephants"—buildings, schools, dams, and machines abandoned by the local populations they were supposed to help.[12]

Sukhomajri's own learning process centered on the puzzle of making the new man-nature configuration *sustainable over time.* Villagers, from an early stage, realized their interest in having a forest management system that could be sustained. But wanting sustainability was not the same thing as doing what was politically necessary to achieve it. That meant confronting hidden forces that had perpetuated village inequities for centuries. In practice, the biggest beneficiaries of Mishra's "bargain" were large landowners who stood to harvest the most crops with the new water. In the region, legal rights to water had traditionally been tied to the amount of land a family owned. Farmers with less land were entitled to less of the new water resource, and some landless to none at all. Not long into Mishra's experiment, it became clear that the poorest villagers had little to gain from the new system, and so little reason to keep their animals off the watershed. The uneven distribution of benefits was, from the start, an open invitation to break the social fence— unless some way could be found to give all villagers a more equal stake in making it work.

Discussions among Mishra, villagers, and social scientists brought in to help,[13] resulted in a plan: Give all families—not just the richer ones—an equal share of the new water supply. Distribution would also be managed by a committee elected by all families.[14] The idea was so outlandish in the northwest Indian context that, even years later, locals like Rameesh Bansar still found its success hard to believe. "Imagine how you would feel if you grew up in this village," he said. "As long as you could remember, the right to own and use water was tied to how much *land* you owned. Now, you're told, every *family* is going to get an equal share, no matter how much, or how little, their land. That's bound to feel strange, even when everyone realizes there may be some wisdom to it."[15]

Sukhomajri appeared to have found its formula for villagewide support. But time brought continued social shocks that no one could have anticipated. Four social scientists—three Indian, one American—worked with villagers to help the experiment adjust. The American was David Seckler, an economist specializing in irrigation projects. In his person Seckler seemed the oddest bedfellow on the Sukhomajri "process team," and much the antithesis of Mishraji. While Mishra, for all his practical bent as a soil and water scientist, was given to heady flights of wonder about the "cosmic energies" released at Sukhomajri, Seckler seemed to relish the more gritty, cynical, and humorous sides of making the new system work. On a side trip from India I searched out Seckler in Jakarta, Indonesia, where he was consulting for the U.S. Agency for International Development. "Sukhomajri shows you've got to be ready for all kinds of unexpected disruptions," he said, leaning back in his office chair. He took a long puff from his cigarette and blew smoke into the air. The wry grin and a worldly cynicism, coupled with rumpled thinning hair, a ruddy complexion, and an open-collared shirt, made for a pleasant combination of hard-headed professional and untamed court jester. For Dave Seckler, the real fun at Sukhomajri didn't come until after the initial success.

"The villagers of Sukhomajri got caught off guard in the first flush of success—they had not yet got down to the hard business of dividing the spoils." Seckler laughed, as if to say this is where things really got interesting. "What followed was a kind of stretching the rules, for a variety of reasons—almost as if people were trying to see how far the system would stretch. For instance, early on it was discovered that the person appointed by the Forestry Department to distribute irrigation water was taking bribes. In exchange for a beer or two, he would let extra water flow into the field of the benefactor. On two other occasions, it was discovered that the irrigation pipes had been broken, dissipating the water. Everybody knew it was caused by a disgruntled villager, but there was no smoking gun found in anyone's hand. These problems were largely resolved once the Water Association was established, along with its rule to give water rights to all families. But even then there was tampering with the pipes. That was when Mishra and I brought outside pressure to bear. We threatened to pull out the irrigation system if villagers did not adhere to the rules. It shows how the learning process can be helped along by a little creative pressure from the outside. Here it worked. The tampering stopped after that."[16]

∎

While David Seckler was in Indonesia, new troubles brewed at Sukhomajri within the village water society itself. R. K. Mukherjee looked on from the inside as the crisis developed. Mukherjee was an Indian development worker in his late 30s. He had worked closely with villagers from the early days. As a staffer for the Society for Promotion of Wastelands Development in New Delhi, he believed that efforts like Sukhomajri's *had* to work if there were to be any hope of reversing land and forest destruction across the subcontinent. Villagers had taken Mukherjee into their confidence as much as he them. "At one point," he said, just days after returning to New Delhi from the village, "I feared that the whole consensus over equal water rights was going to collapse, breaking the social fence altogether." Mukherjee was a tall, sturdy individual, though conciliatory in demeanor—just the sort of person one might expect to be called in to mediate a crisis. "None of us could have anticipated this flap over equal rights," he explained. "Village leaders had affirmed the principle so strongly."

The first solution devised by villagers to ensure equal benefits involved a coupon system. Each family received an equal number of coupons. They could then choose whether to cash in their coupons for irrigation water or sell them to other families for cash. In this way, each family would be assured equal benefits. "At first the system worked like a charm," said Mukherjee. "But over time it foundered. Larger landholders became disgruntled. Before, they'd had very few business dealings with smallholders. Now they found themselves having to deal with precisely those people, bargaining for the water they wanted. Their frustration got serious. Meanwhile, the spread of coupons into the hands of so many people was getting unwieldy. Villagers were frustrated over the absence of a central marketplace for water. When I arrived just days ago the entire distribution system was tottering on the brink."

The tension on Mukherjee's face eased. "Once again the water society took up debate, and once again their solution is, I think, remarkable. It's remarkable because, on the face of it, the principle of equality was relaxed; but from another point of view, the outcome may be more sustainable over time. The coupon system will now be dropped, and a central marketplace for water purchases set up—again managed by the Water Association." Previously, the Association's job was simply to distribute coupons each year to the families. All transactions were carried out between the families themselves. Now the

Association will sell water directly to families according to need. "This does compromise the equal benefits principle but doesn't eliminate it altogether," Mukherjee insisted. "The new system essentially creates a central marketplace where larger landholders—who need more than their family's quota would allow—can buy the extra water they need. This eliminates dealings they find awkward with smallholders. The Association will still be elected by all families. The system also had a simplicity that is much more workable. And the Association will spend the money from its water sales on school facilities and other public improvements that will benefit the village as a whole. So families with little land will benefit directly, though they no longer get coupon cash each year. They still have a stake in making the system work."[17]

■

By the time Sukhomajri's water governance system settled down, in the late 1980s, the experiment had been more than ten years in the making. Its rule of spreading benefits to all families—first conceived in the early '80s—took five years to gain acceptance in its modified form. As a villager put it, "That's the time it takes for change to be accepted here. Then people get used to it, it becomes law." But beyond needing time, Sukhomajri had to be ready to redefine change, even after the first new threads of change had settled around the social body. One set of adjustments led to the next. The next, too, needed time to settle. And so the learning process took on a continuing life of its own.[18]

The ultimate test of "elegance" for Sukhomajri's learning process would be its replicability elsewhere. From an early stage, planners saw in the experiment a model applicable to problems all across the foothills. In fact, by the mid-1980s the model had already been tried in a nearby village, with some success.[19] Mishra and his colleagues spent no little time taking the good news to officials in New Delhi, urging replication on a much wider scale. From 1983 through 1988 their appeal stirred no response in the halls of power, despite recommendations from blue-ribbon panels and studies showing that over 600 sites were ideal for Sukhomajri-like transformation.[20] Those responsible for national water and forestry programs had not been directly involved in Sukhomajri's success and so were reluctant to back something for which they could not claim direct credit. Even when replication was considered, bureaucratic disputes ensued over which government department would take the lead.

Just as replication of the Sukhomajri model appeared to be smothering in bureaucratic quicksand, its magic revived. Early in 1989 national planners gave the green light for replication in dozens of sites across northern India. Mishra had, by then, given up waiting and started some self-appointed replication of his own. Traveling to the other side of India, to wastelands in his home state of Bihar, he started talking once again with villagers, some of whom he had known from youth. On long journeys by foot, Mishra accompanied villagers on their daily walks into restricted state forestland, searching for more trees to cut. He asked questions, the kinds he had always asked: "Have you ever thought of exchanging what you now do for a living for something better? Did you realize you can harvest much, much more from nature while actually helping it to thrive? Why, when our earth has such abundant sunshine and such abundant water, is everyone living in such poverty?"

1. Marcus Franda, "Conservation, Water and Human Development at Sukhomajri" (American Universities Field Staff Reports, 1981, No. 13). The pressure of population growth on natural resources in the Himalayan hills may pose even more serious problems in the years ahead. One study, by J. C. Nautiyal and P. S. Babor in 1984, estimated that if hill population continues to increase at its (then) current rate, all afforestable land (village forests and reserve forests) would be required by the year 2025 to meet the need for fodder and firewood (cited in Kamla Chowdhry et al., "Hill Resource Development and Community Management: Lessons Learnt on Micro-watershed Management from the Cases of Sukhomajri and Dasholi Gram Swarajya Mandal," [mimeo. report submitted to the Indian Planning Commission's Working Group on Hill Area Development, August 1984], p. 36).

2. By the 1970s yearly topsoil loss had reached 200 tons per acre, according to workers based at the Chandigarh branch of the Central Soil and Water Conservation Research and Training Institute.

3. For a broad discussion of social forestry issues, see Michael M. Cernea, "User Groups as Producers in Participatory Afforestation Strategies," World Bank Discussion Paper No. 70 (Washington, DC: World Bank, 1989). Explaining the rather serendipitous way in which this "bargain" originated, the Ford Foundation's Norman R. Collins writes, "The dam was built at the outset as a water conservation structure, to hold back the runoff to avoid erosion that was damaging the lake below. The dam was not built as a water storage device for irrigation, as evidenced by the fact that when the dam was built there was only a rather imperfectly constructed spillway for surplus water to avoid breaking the dam—not an outlet to channel water to the fields below. It was only later that various of the minds (within the Ford Foundation, the [Central Soil and Water Conservation Research and Training] Center and among the

farmers) came to the bright idea that perhaps the water could be used beneficially for something—like irrigation. When the water was so used, it then came quite naturally to the villagers that it made sense to protect the hills so that the dam would not silt up" (Correspondence to the author, April 12, 1990). Another development worker involved in the project, Madhu Sarin, indicates that the villagers themselves might have originated the irrigation idea once they saw that the dams built to break erosion were actually holding water (Interview, November 1989, with Madhu Sarin, Cambridge, MA).

4. Franda (op. cit., p. 5) wrote of P. R. Mishra in 1981: "Mishra is an unusual director for a scientific project in India, if only because he has no advanced degrees and is one of the least officious persons one could meet. But whoever named Mishra director of the [Central Soil and Water Conservation Research and Training Institute] research station at Chandigarh knew what he was doing. The son and grandson of high-school teachers, Mishra was born in Bihar nearly six decades ago, fell in love with forestry at an early age, and has been actively engaged in it since his teens. He has obvious competence in the wide variety of disciplines involved in successful soil and water conservation activities, plus a unique ability to relate to villagers. As one walks around the watersheds near Sukhomajri with him it is clear that he knows every plant, every engineering device, and almost every person in the area."

5. The dilemma of poor villagers like those at Sukhomajri is explained by economist David Seckler, formerly of Colorado State University and consultant to the Sukhomajri experiment in its early phases: "These people cannot save resources for the future through reduced current consumption, nor can they direct resources from present production to invest in increased future production. Savings, or investment, is the difference between income and consumption. When people consume all their income, and even then consumption is only at subsistence levels, they cannot be expected to save and invest until their income is increased. . . . [All attempts to promote conservation by diverting] resources from current production—controlled grazing, fruit tree planting, exhortations not to cultivate 'lands unsuitable for agriculture,' failed for lack of village cooperation and, at times, outright opposition. On the other hand, development programs with an immediate payoff commanded the enthusiastic support of the villagers. . . . Once villagers have a productive resource in hand, they will indeed conserve this resource to the best of their ability" (David Seckler & Deep Joshi, "Sukhomajri: A Rural Development Program in India," [New Delhi: Prepared for the Ford Foundation, 1981], mimeo., pp. 2–3). For a more detailed assessment of the Sukhomajri experiment by Seckler, see "Institutionalism and Agricultural Development In India," *Journal of Economic Issues* 20(4), Dec. 1986.

6. As late as the 1980s, Sukhomajri-like approaches to conservation stood in stark contrast to many longstanding policies of government conservation agencies, according to Cornell irrigation specialist Gilbert Levine, who spent several years in the mid-1980s studying a variety of Indian water schemes similar to Sukhomajri's. "The prevailing tradition in government conservation organizations," he said, "comes largely from the German tradition of forestry. There you have forest guards and a protectionist view that tries to minimize use of the forest resources. Sukhomajri-like approaches, on the other hand, reason that the people are there, they have to have some way to live, so how can resources be managed in a way that will yield some optimal mix of resource use and protection? The two approaches require very different systems of training and have a very different set of measures as to what constitutes success" (Telephone interview, March 1988).

7. Changes in production between 1975 and 1981 were described, though not

with extensive scientific documentation, in a report prepared in 1984 for the Indian Planning Commission's Working Group on Hill Area Development (Chowdhry, op. cit., pp. 8, 28). The report indicated, among other things, that the availability of new water for irrigation made possible an increase in crop rotations from two to four, depending on the choice of farmers. Between 1977 and 1981, the production rose from 250 quintals of wheat to 1,015, from 500 quintals of wheat straw to 2,031, from 196 quintals of maize to 356, and from 2,196 liters of milk to 4,405. Meanwhile the rate of grass production in the water catchment area increased from 200 kilograms per acre per year to 2,500. (In the neighboring village of Nada, where a Sukhomajri-style experiment was also tried, the planting of new grasses across the hills made possible a lucrative rope-weaving industry.) Franda reported (op. cit., p. 8) that by 1981 the new water resources at Sukhomajri had made possible the adoption of high-yield seeds and chemical fertilizers. Over three quarters of the farmers were using chemical fertilizers and improved varieties of wheat or maize, and more than half the village lands were being sown with high-yield seeds. Perhaps the most important result, however, was the great improvement in the farmer's ability to control and predict the availability of water. After a failure of rains in 1979, for instance, Sukhomajri's maize crop was saved at the end of the growing season by reservoir water. (For some cost-benefit assessments of the technological change at Sukhomajri, see Seckler and Joshi, op. cit., Appendix 1.)

8. While the centrality of environmental concerns was attaining prominence in rural areas of the developing world, in the 1980s it was also gaining recognition with regard to agriculture in industrialized countries. The experience of some working farms in the North persuaded a growing number of scientists that environmentally sound agriculture can equal the productivity of high-cost, high-chemical methods. In America, Rodale International pioneered such methods. European nations like Norway were developing a variety of demonstration farms with 100 percent chemical-free farming.

9. Michael Redclift, *Sustainable Development: Exploring the Contradictions* (London: Methuen, 1987), pp. 32–36. This is a good overview of sustainability issues. For a more technical discussion of the factors involved in analyzing the integration of agriculture and the ecosystem, see Gordon R. Conway, *Agroecosystem Analysis for Research and Development* (Bangkok: Winrock International, 1986).

10. As early as 1980, the Sukhomajri water scheme had liberated the village from dependence on outside sources of food and from the fear of sudden shortages. As was reported at that time, "The recommended energy consumption for India is 2,200 kcal per person per day, or roughly ⅔ kg of wheat, or its equivalent. At 240 kg per capita per year the 455 people at Sukhomajri need 109,200 kg per annum; 48,000 kg per annum, or about one-half of their total annual requirement, is provided by the *additional* rabi wheat production [made possible by the water scheme] alone" (Seckler and Joshi, op. cit., Appendix 1, p. 4).

11. In the language of management theory, agricultural economist David Seckler called it "management by results," as opposed to the traditional "management by objectives" (Seckler, op. cit., p. 1022). Korten's phrase derives from his article, D. C. Korten, "Community Organizations and Rural Development: A Learning Process Approach," *Public Administration Review* 40(5):480–511. A learning process approach is critical for change in the management of commonly held natural resources—so-called common property. Experience has shown that such change frequently turns up unanticipated factors that impinge further on the management system. Garrett Hardin, in 1968, brought into focus the dilemma associated with many common-property sys-

tems. When one person extracts something for "private" benefit (such as grazing animals over a commons that has limited grasses), the cost is shared by the "collective" society because resources left for others are thereby depleted. Individuals tend not to put collective interests above their private interests, thus threatening the natural resource base for quite logical reasons of personal survival ("The Tragedy of the Commons," *Science* 162 [1968]: pp. 1243–48). In a case like Sukhomajri, the practice may continue until economic production declines. New rules are then put in place to restrict access to the common property (the grazing lands), and a new equilibrium is reached. But, as Cornell's Gilbert Levine points out, it is difficult at that stage to know how forces will impinge on the new system. "No one can predict how well the adjustments will work, particularly if there are insiders or outsiders who realize the new system is yielding rewards, and want to acquire some of those rewards. So the importance of taking a learning process approach is based on the recognition that you simply don't know what will happen after a change in management. You have to monitor things to find out" (Interview cited above).

12. See Introduction for an example of how inadequate understanding of local conditions in Nigeria led to an unfortunate attempt to transfer Iowan farm technology to that country.

13. The "learning process team" was hired with the help of grants from the Ford Foundation. It included Madhu Sarin, a development worker from Chandigarh; Deep Joshi, an Indian management consultant trained at the Massachusetts Institute of Technology; David Seckler, an agricultural economist from Colorado State University; and R. K. Mukherjee, a wastelands redevelopment consultant from New Delhi. Sukhomajri was clearly fortunate to have external funding to support its learning process component.

14. The Water Users' Association first received authority from the Central Soil and Water Research and Conservation Institute to manage the village water scheme in 1980. The Association comprised all water users, and was headed by a committee of ten village leaders, P. R. Mishra, and S. P. Malhotra, a former engineer-in-chief of the Irrigation Department of Haryana. The World Bank's Michael Cernea points out that no one type of social group will be appropriate for all resource management activities; different tasks will require different types of village-based associations and sets of actors in order for activities to be sustained over time (op. cit., pp. 25–66).

15. This also meant some eventual reconstruction of the irrigation system. Initially, the very way the pipes were laid left out half the villagers, which, according to development worker Madhu Sarin, created terrible conflict among them and increased the pressure for more equal distribution (Interview, November 1989).

16. Seckler recalls a humorous incident when disciplinary action was required from project outsiders. To get more than his share of water, a farmer had dug down to the water pipe and poked a hole in it, "but since the water was under pressure he could not turn it off. We let it run a few days before fixing the leak. This not only provided condign punishment through moderate flood damage to this farmer's field, but perhaps more important, made him something of a laughingstock in the village. That was the first and last breakage of the pipe" (op. cit., pp. 1025–26). Seckler argues very strongly that social pressure from within the village would not alone have been sufficient to enforce the new social forestry and water distribution systems. "I contend that effective legal systems are a necessary condition to any kind of economic development.... Thus ... we made sure that the right of the households to water was a legal right and that it would be legally enforced through the agency of the outsider on the board of the [water users' association] if necessary. The 'invisible

control' exercised by the law was, in my opinion, absolutely indispensable to the success of the [water users' association]. It would not have worked simply through 'social pressure'.... Looking back I believe that control of the positive feedback through this dual system redundancy [enforcing change through *both* social pressure and legal control] was the single most important factor in the success of Sukhomajri" (op. cit., p. 1024). Process team member Madhu Sarin described the importance of outsider help in mediating early disputes: "We would insist every time there was any conflict, 'Let us all get together.... We will be present as neutral outsiders, but you better sort this out. Let's get others to come in and vouch for your statements. But ultimately you have got to learn to solve these conflicts yourselves.' [Without this kind of external pressure there arose] suspicions that [until a new tradition of villagewide supervision came into play] three or four guys who were controlling the management committee could misappropriate some of the funds" (Interview, November 1989).

17. The exact social effects of eliminating the coupon system and making the Association a "marketplace" for water purchases would ultimately need to be assessed through empirical investigation. Some might argue that the change brought greater dominance of water resources by the richer, more powerful farmers, to the detriment of worse-off farmers. The original coupon system had made it possible not only for all families to gain equal "water cash," but also for landless villagers to exchange their coupons for the right to work small tracts of land, sharing produce with the owners. Some sharecropping arrangements begun under the coupon system continued after the system was dropped, but to whose advantage—tenants or landlords—is unclear. Most project planners agree, however, that even after the coupon system ended, the water scheme embodied equality-enhancing principles. "Even if you are convinced that a village's resource distribution system will benefit from greater equality," explained project consultant Deep Joshi, "in all practicality you may need to change your initial ideas about how that equality should be achieved. At Sukhomajri we began with total equality and evolved to a system based on less than equal distribution. But this does not mean that we, or the villagers, lost concern for equality. It means that we needed to follow a course that was practical under the circumstances, and in keeping with the villagers' own sense of fairness. Fairness may often be judged according to standards that differ from perfect equality. So ultimately one needs to be flexible, open to solutions that are practical under the circumstances, and which people themselves agree to be fair" (Interview, January 1986, with Deep Joshi in New Delhi).

18. Process team member Madhu Sarin also followed the effects of change on women. She observed that newfound prosperity introduced new burdens for women. As the fields and hills fruited with new crops and fodder, so did the workload of women increase—to gather them. In addition, women began to participate more generally in the commerce of village life, introducing certain strains on the traditional expectations of men and family. A second-generation problem of critical import was how women would sort out these tensions and strains. The women of Sukhomajri, said Ms. Sarin, would never trade their new situation for the old, since their new economic prosperity had made life psychologically so much more secure. But by the late 1980s the learning process had to go much further (Madhu Sarin, April 1989, interviewed on film in Sukhomajri by the staff of World Development Productions, Inc., Cambridge, MA). These changes for women are elaborated at the opening of Chapter Eight.

19. With financial assistance from the Ford Foundation, planners first demonstrated that the model could be adapted to the conditions of Nada, a village about 15

kilometers from Sukhomajri. There a Sukhomajri-like approach proved quite lucrative for the villagers, including those who belonged to a subcommunity of untouchables. A new industry, the weaving of rope from tall grasses that spread across the hills once the grazing stopped, greatly improved the income-earning capacity of women.

20. In 1984 a subcommittee of the Commission's Working Group on Hill Area Development heartily recommended greater national investment in Sukhomajri-like projects, arguing that it not be made on the narrow basis of bankability, but rather on the basis of the exponential, regionwide benefits such investment brings (Chowdhry, op. cit., pp. 28–29). Project planners also began discussions with the U.S. Agency for International Development to explore the funding of hundreds of similar projects. But replication foundered, partly because of the difficulty in finding the right agencies to carry it out. Plans were considered, but abandoned, for the administration of replication by private development agencies. Another possible executor would be an existing government department, whether irrigation, forestry, or conservation. During the bureaucratic confusion of 1987, Cornell's Gilbert Levine explains a decision to delegate replication to these agencies was simply not, bureaucratically speaking, easy for the Indian government. "When agencies were set up to do reforestation and build dams, their scientists and engineers were charged with stopping erosion, not with integrating conservation with economic change. To get these agencies to link their conservation mandate with social interests required major changes, including the involvement of social scientists in the agencies themselves—something like trying to introduce social scientists into the U.S. Army Corps of Engineers. Actually some such changes *have* taken place in the Corps of Engineers, but only very gradually, and with some considerable difficulty. There's no reason why we in America should expect more rapid changes from the Indian government than we do of our own." Studies by Levine and his colleagues determined that, "out of some 3,000 dams already in place in the foothills, as many as 600 may be suitable to Sukhomajri-like efforts" (Interview, October 1988, with Gilbert Levine).

8

Late-breaking Insights for Change: Women, Hunger, and High-tech in Gandhi Country

ANAND, INDIA

Six hundred miles south of Sukhomajri, on the west side of India, is the state of Gujarat. There, not far from the site of Gandhi's first campaigns of nonviolent resistance, is the headquarters of a program acclaimed in the 1980s as one of the biggest and most successful development strategies in the world—the AMUL Dairy. Using advanced technology and management skills, the Dairy linked the milk production of vast numbers of villagers—most of them women—with urban markets, virtually doubling the income of rural households. But the Dairy's success in making breadwinners of village women was followed by new demands from those same women, revealing serious problems no one had taken into account. AMUL Dairy confronted the choice: Should it, or should it not, respond?

October 17, 1989. Dignitaries begin to gather at the National Museum of Natural History in Washington, DC. Rumors have been circulating for weeks, but now the recipient of the 1989 World Food Prize—the "Nobel" of food and agriculture—will be announced. The auditorium fills to capacity as more and more ambassadors, politicians, and development professionals arrive. The lights drop. From behind the stage a large screen descends, a film begins to roll, and a narrator's voice is heard. "Verghese Kurien has unleashed the energy within the Indian people and changed the life of the average Indian farmer. A cycle of poverty has been broken."[1]

■

I first began following the career of Verghese Kurien in 1978, after interviewing him at the World Bank in Washington, DC. He had just come out of the office of the Bank's president, Robert S. McNamara. Kurien had a way of thinking big, asking big, and getting what he wanted. With McNamara it was a quick loan of $150 million to launch a new phase of his dairy revolution in India—the so-called White Revolution. Only a few weeks before he had persuaded the European community to give, as an outright gift, $250 million worth of surplus milk powder. This he would convert into liquid milk, "flood" the markets of major Indian cities, and use the income to further expand India's own internal dairy operations. It was the second time Kurien had sought milk powder from abroad to prime India's dairy pump. The first effort started the process of linking rural milk producers in 18 major "milksheds," or collection areas, with urban consumers in Delhi, Calcutta, Madras, and Bombay. With his new revenues Kurien now planned to extend milk marketing to over 400 cities from 164 milksheds. If all went as expected, by the late '80s over 5 million milk producers would be involved. An average of 10 million kilograms of milk would be collected every day. As the first expansion had taken the code name "Operation Flood," the new expansion would be "Operation Flood II."

Some of the greatest beneficiaries of Flood II would be the thousands upon thousands of village women who had always done much of the work in Indian dairying, but got relatively little attention. They were the ones who milked and cared for village cows and buffalos, transporting the milk to collection sites for delivery to processing plants. The cash they received on delivery fetched a much-needed income supplement for the household. With the addition of a steady and certain cash flow each day, rural households no longer would have to depend so heavily on money the husband brought home only once each year at harvest time. In a country of village families with a long tradition of milk production, Kurien's plan for linking producers with modern processing plants and urban markets had an appropriateness that could readily take hold on a mass scale and be sustained over time.

"Malnutrition is a function of poverty," he had said back in 1978 at the start of Operation Flood II. "The answer to malnutrition is increasing *income*, giving people something to do to earn more. Operation Flood is the greatest nutritional project in the world—not because it produces more food, but because it doubles the income of millions of families. With this, poor people can buy the food they need." In the years that followed, Kurien not only expanded AMUL Dairy in the western state of Gujarat, but transformed national dairy operations into one of the largest in the world, ranking India third in milk production after the United States and the Soviet Union. He transported refrigerated milk by rail from his headquarters in Gujarat all the way across India to Calcutta, one of the longest milk-shipping operations in the world. As dairying operations reached that magnitude, Kurien's claims to be making a dent in rural poverty, and so malnutrition, could not be ignored.

Not all observers saw so humanitarian a motive in the emergence of the dairy movement. Some characterized it more as an attempt, starting in the early 1950s, to end a growing dependence of India on dairy products from U.S. foreign aid and European multinationals like Nestle.[2] In its early years AMUL unquestionably *did* draw momentum from the "Quit Britain" movements of the 1930s and '40s and from popular aspirations for national self-reliance. Some of the main backers of dairy expansion in the 1950s were lead players in the independence movement, men like Morarji Desai, Sardar Patel, and Tribhuvandas Patel.[3] But whatever the early motivations of dairy expansion, AMUL Dairy and Operation Flood eventually gave new prominence to forgotten factors in the hunger equation— women. They were not merely "farmers' wives," Kurien argued, but needed to be understood as breadwinners in their own right. If you put more income in the hands of women, he said, you transform the household economy and reduce hunger. It was an idea that, by the 1980s, had also gained acceptance worldwide among agencies trying to reduce hunger and malnutrition. A proposition long understood by development agencies like UNICEF was, by now, common wisdom: When women get opportunities to earn income and are allowed to spend it, the money generally goes for child nutrition and care for the vulnerable members of society, whereas men often spend new income on a new shirt or a night on the town.[4] Moreover, from the early '80s, social science surveys had been showing that remunerative employment and education for women may pay dividends in reducing global population pressure. In impoverished areas large family size was traditionally viewed as the only insurance policy a family could have. When the household economy improved, when women got more control over income, and when economic security increased in the broader society, women in many countries indicated a desire to have smaller, better-educated families.[5] As the recognition of the importance of women grew in the 1980s, so did interest in Kurien's dairy scheme, not just for its implications for India, but worldwide.

It was not at all clear just how "women-oriented development" would play itself out in various life settings around the world. Efforts to help women earn more for their labor were precipitating a wide variety of social conflicts and responses from women themselves. At Sukhomajri village in northern India (Chapter Seven), development workers worried that the same advances that made some things better for women also made some things worse. On the one hand, local prosperity made all villagers more secure, including women. But it also meant a much greater workload for women, the ones who had to harvest new crops and cut new hill fodder to feed the animals. Development worker Madhu Sarin had no doubt that rising economic well-being in the village had its benefits for women. "They would not trade the present for the past," she said, "for psychologically they are much, much more secure." But Ms. Sarin also criticized village leaders for continuing to exclude women from village governance, even on matters that deeply affected them. As persons affected by village transformations, she argued, women needed to play a more active role in decision making, or the Sukhomajri experiment would not really succeed in the long run.[6]

The women benefiting from the expansion of AMUL Dairy operations were also said to have their complaints about the course of events. Something, they said, had got out of balance. More attention was paid to servicing the giant milk production system than the fundamental systems of human well-being. "If your buffalo gets sick," the saying went, "you can get a doctor overnight. If your child gets sick, you'll be lucky to get one in four months." Seasoned observers of the Dairy were becoming concerned that attention had shifted from helping the poor to replicating the organization.[7] As village women were now pressing the Dairy with new concerns, so was the Dairy said to be seeking new ways to respond. But to what extent could such a massive bureaucratized program be expected to adjust midstream? As I left Sukhomajri and headed for Gujarat state in early 1988, I sought to learn more.

■

Anyone who travels in India will inevitably encounter, in one form or another, the influence of AMUL Dairy. Get stuck in a traffic jam on your way to Delhi's airport and your eyes light on AMUL's blue-and-white milkdrop symbol painted on the wall of a milk dispensary beside the road—one of thousands across the city. Dozens of people with large decanters wait in queue to pick up their daily milk. Or, once your flight leaves the ground, a lunch tray arrives from your Air India hostess bearing patties of AMUL butter, replete with foil wrapping sporting the classic milkdrop symbol. By the late 1980s Indians themselves did not think twice about the widespread availability of AMUL products—it was assumed, although it hadn't always been. The Dairy's urban marketing of milk, butter, cheeses, and other products now extended nationwide. If some curiosity remained about AMUL, it was the way the Dairy still based its high-tech industrial operations in the state where Mahatma Gandhi, India's supreme low-tech advocate, first challenged the captains of industry.

In Ahmedabad, one of the largest cities of Gujarat state, the spirit of Gandhi lost none of its grip on the public mind. Memories of the struggles to overcome fear when facing British guns, the confrontations with textile mills over working conditions, the campaigns for one-person, one-vote democracy—all had congealed into a subconscious, but persistent, set of expectations that pervaded daily life. The struggles begun at Ahmedabad gave life to the idea that the "little guy" counts, even in a nation of 700 million little guys, most living in the countryside. Without the impetus of those struggles, it is hard to imagine how village India could have embraced the concept of one-person, one-vote, to lay a foundation for the largest system of democratic elections on earth. Over the centuries village governance had never really been democratic. The panchayats, or village councils, were automatically ruled by people of social and economic rank, of higher caste and older in years, and only rarely of lower caste. Independence changed all that. Now village councils were elected on the basis of one-person, one-vote.[8] In the state of Gujarat, most all of the "little guys" who got the right to vote also just happened to own a milch cow, or two.

On the outskirts of Ahmedabad, the Gandhi *ashram* still looked
out over the Sabarmati River, as it always had done. In a cluster of
simple shelters and shade trees the "Great Soul" had gathered with
associates to undergo spiritual disciplines and plan political strategy.
The simplicity of the ashram was a loud rejection of modernity, or
modernity as much twentieth-century architecture defined it. The
main building was a large platform enclosed on three sides and covered by a roof that rested on simple square columns, the open side
looking out across a lazy shallow river. Still visible from the platform were the smokestacks of Ahmedabad textile plants, whose foul
working conditions and low wages were some of Gandhi's first tar-
gets of protest in 1918. Modern society, Gandhi believed, could do
without much industrialization and still achieve a high order of
civilization. He conceded that some "key industries" might be necessary, and did not necessarily oppose machinery or the formation of
productive capital and markets. But reviving India, as he saw it,
fundamentally meant reaffirming the value of simple labor, small
cottage industries, and "noble living," while resisting the onrush of
consumerism.[9] Gandhi was concerned partly with meeting the
needs of vast numbers of village-based people without taking from
them the fruits of their labor, as industrial production often did.[10] He
was also trying to cope with hard choices posed by imbalances in the
Indian development equation: too many people, mostly in the countryside, and too many aspirations that could not be met in the near
term even with the most favorable industrial growth. Now that independence had arrived, where would India's priorities be placed?
Would those who were already better-off, a minority living in the
cities, capture the lion's share of progress? Gandhi's own measure of
success in development began with the extent to which benefits
reached poor people and minorities, including those at the very bottom of the social totem pole—the Harijans, or untouchables. As one
principle of the ashram put it, "Untouchability, which has taken
such deep root in Hinduism, is altogether irreligious. Its removal has
therefore been treated as an independent principle. The so-called
untouchables have equal place in the ashram with other classes."
Women, too, should have more rights in the social order of the
future, including remuneration for their labor. "In the new order of
my imagination, all will work according to their capacity for an

adequate return. . . . Women in the new order will be part-time work-ers, their primary function being to look after the home."[11]

In the aftermath of Gandhi's campaigns, not far to the south of his Ahmedabad ashram another model of "helping the little guy" would be tested by Verghese Kurien and a group of nationalist leaders who had worked with Gandhi in the "Quit Britain" campaigns.[12] This time industrialization would not be cautioned against, but rather exploited to the hilt. It was possible, the new theory went, to reverse the pattern of industrial lords dominating the little guy and to bring the technocrats to the little guy's service. First, establish democrati-cally governed milk cooperatives comprised of villagers who own milch cows; then set up a modern plant to process village milk and market it to the big cities; finally, hire professionals to manage the plant and have leaders regularly elected by the village coop members. Then you would have a system responsible to the members, for it would be owned *by* them. At a time when Maoist China or Castro's Cuba had considerable success reducing hunger through centralized "command" economies, Kurien set forth a decentralized, demo-cratic model. Perhaps here in the heart of Gandhi country, there was no other way a reformer, even a technocrat like Kurien, could go.[13] "One of the principal obstacles to progress in the developing world," he had said in 1985, "is the centralized power of governmental bu-reaucracies. They fear being accountable to village people. But in our country people in the countryside are basically good people; many of lesser character go to the cities for money and power. The rural people live close to the land, they are basically good. To unleash the power of these people, to give that power direction and thrust, you need an Operation Flood, you need professional managers. This is the role in which I cast myself—how to give direction and thrust to this undoubtedly good thing of India, this enormously powerful thing, the heart of its people. In my view development means com-bining the good rural energies with professional management for guidance and direction."[14]

The sun was rising as I drove by car from Ahmedabad to dairy headquarters in Anand. The road, like the land, was monotonously flat, though lined along many stretches with trees that break the beams of morning sun into a strobe-light effect across the highway. The surrounding flatlands, like most of western India, were stripped

John Schal

of their forests, leaving open farmlands to bake day after day in the tropical sun. Village after village evidenced the apparent workability of Kurien's "theory." Women in brilliantly colored saris performed their bi-daily ritual, making their way by foot to local milk collection stations, balancing on their heads large metal jugs that gleamed in the sun. My guide, V. H. Shah, had long experience in dairying. "I still find it awesome" he said, "when I realize this same ritual plays itself out in thousands of villages all over India." If one could imagine an Indian David Niven, V. H. Shah would be he, with his slicked-back hair, square jaw, squint eyes, boxer's nose, and thin brown mustache clinging to the ridge of his upper lip. His look of free-wheeling confidence was complemented by the informality of his spread-collar shirt, tan khakis, and striped green sweater. "What is still so striking for me after all these years," he said, "is the fact that these villagers from all castes come to the milk collection stations. They stand together in the same lines, pouring all their milk into the same can—including the untouchables. This system is more than an orderly way to collect milk; it's a blow to the caste system. It doesn't matter if you're an untouchable or a Brahmin—whoever gets to the line first stands first."[15]

Over the years, the "Anand Pattern" had acquired a fame of near mythical proportions. Not a few cynics had come to the milk processing headquarters at Anand prepared to tear down "the myth." But to approach the sixty-acre dairy complex was to become, if not a believer, at least considerably impressed. The headquarters building was a spread of white concrete, about twenty-five meters high, fifty meters long. In the foreground lay a circular pool and fountain, surrounded at the perimeter by blooming flowers. The headquarters housed the whole gamut of dairy operations, from receiving and pasteurizing incoming milk, to processing it into cheese and chocolate for sale. Across the parking lot, workers dressed in white shorts, white shirts, and white caps pushed large trolleys stacked with milk jars. At the gate hundreds of village women stepped out of buses and a parade of tanker trucks arrived with the day's unprocessed milk. Above the headquarters roof loomed the tops of silolike milk storage tanks and aerial walkways arching over railroad cars. V. H. Shah pointed to the astonishment on the faces of village women. "Remember," he said, "these are the people who own this operation. Think of what it must mean to a village woman when she first sees all the gleaming steel vats, the workers, the railroad cars, the trucks, and realizes, 'I own a piece of all this.' Many of these women had never before gone out of their village; now they're standing in front of a corporate headquarters their local milk societies actually *own*."

■

From an early stage Verghese Kurien was concerned that women step forward and play a more active role, not just in collecting milk but in running the cooperatives. Women eventually *did* step forward, but not in ways Kurien originally had hoped. By the late 1970s—more than two decades into the White Revolution—few women were getting involved in the local management committees. Far more were involved in pressing other demands to dairy headquarters. The new income from milk, they complained, was not doing nearly enough for household nutrition and health. The complaint seemed to contradict a long-held view at the Dairy that raising incomes would end hunger and malnutrition in the countryside. Despite some striking success in raising household income, village women now argued that some critical factors in the Indian hunger equation were still missing. A short drive from dairy headquarters at Anand, I was told, AMUL's sole woman veterinarian might shed some light.

V. H. Shah arranged for transport to an outdoor buffalo stable where Dr. Sarojiniben Nair was teaching village women about animal husbandry. True to AMUL's high-tech reputation, Dr. Nair and the veterinarian staff used only the latest techniques in animal care and propagation, including artificial insemination and the storage of frozen buffalo sperm in nitrogen-cooled containers that could be shipped out for use in the villages. For the techniques to be applied at the village level, however, the women who would use them had to see firsthand how the "AI" (artificial insemination) principles worked. For many, the outdoor training sessions would be their first encounter with the idea that a female buffalo can be impregnated without physical contact with a male. Beyond AI, women at the village level would learn about handling milk, especially the importance of not diluting it before taking it to collection sites. For years women were ignorant of the dangers of watering down the milk's fat content, and thought dilution the simple way to increase the volume of the milk they would deliver to AMUL. Only with education, and the provision of electric fat-testing machines at collection stations, did the diluting stop.

V. H. Shah led the way to a large tent-canopy where Dr. Nair was completing her talk to a crowd of village women. "While we have many women instructors," he said, "Dr. Nair is the first woman to join the professional veterinarian staff. Compared with men, there is a huge difference in the rapport Dr. Nair has with the women. She connects with them. The gents seem to create distance, to push their authority." In her late 30s, Dr. Nair was wearing a white sari with a light-blue floral pattern. Unlike the village women, she did not wear the sari up over her head—a practice often dispensed with by more educated Indian women. "We've found we can teach ladies

much more than the gents," she explained. "Before, it was assumed that you would just teach the gents and they would, in turn, share information with the women. But this never really worked. Seeing is believing, and those who *do the work* of animal care—the ladies—must do the learning directly. It also isn't easy for ladies to be taught by gents about things like AI—they're shy, a little embarrassed when the gents are there. It hints at how delicate the relationship is between men and women, and a caution women feel about upsetting that relationship. This may help to explain why more women do not come forward to take leadership roles in the dairy councils." Dr. Nair paused as she pulled the strap of her purse over her shoulder.

"But it's a mistake to think that women are not willing to come forward at all," she said. "It's *significant* that they pressed the Dairy so strongly for education in household nutrition and health. This may be the avenue they think best to pursue just now. And they did get the organization to respond. That joke about buffalos getting more care than children—it's had a real impact. The women's demand for education could not be ignored, and a whole program of education in nutrition and health was set up—the Tribhuvandas Foundation. I think it's a credit to the Dairy that it was willing to move in this direction, even so late in its history.[16] But it may also suggest that ladies are actually coming forward more than many people think."

Not far from the outdoor "classroom" where Dr. Nair taught animal care, village women were getting education of a different sort. There, at a center in Rajodpura village, the Tribhuvandas Foundation had set up its health and nutrition programs with the help of funding from one of the grand old men of the independence movement, Tribhuvandas K. Patel, as well as UNICEF, Britain's Overseas Development Administration, and AMUL Dairy itself. At the classroom in a cluster of shade trees, nutrition and child health classes were under way. Some instructors showed how grinding up a combination of nuts and grains could provide a highly nutritious, high-protein meal for children. Others explained principles of sanitation and encouraged women to use environmentally sound cooking practices, including energy-efficient, smokeless cookers fueled by biogas. The center's training in basic health and nutrition was also being shared in the field through mobile health care training teams moving from village to village.[17]

Outside the classroom, a poor woman strolled slowly with her sobbing two-year-old son, Narayan. Raji Patel had brought him to the center just fifteen days before, in hopes he could be saved from diarrhea and dehydration. Narayan now took tentative steps on Foundation grounds, leaning forward on a four-leg walker. He winced with pain at every step, his swelled stomach bulging out of his shirt. "We had almost given up," said Mrs. Patel. "He had become all skin and bones, his stomach swelling up, and he couldn't hold liquids. While the center has been giving him oral rehydration therapy and foods, I am learning how to make those foods and keep things clean." In fact, all along, ending the protein deficiency that took the lives of countless children had been as close at hand as mixing a simple combination of readily available local crops—wheat, peanuts, and gram (a leguminous plant of the same family as the chickpea). Ending the dehydration that took so many more lives was as easy as mixing sugar and salts in clean water—a formula widely disseminated by UNICEF.[18] Yet until now, such techniques had remained a mystery to village women, even those with many a milk rupee in their pockets.

■

The traditions of Hindu lore consistently affirm the importance of the stage of life known as *grihastha,* or householding. Yet there have long been tensions and contradictions in the way the traditions portray women's role and status in the household. Sometimes the woman is seen as equal in status to the man, sometimes unequal, and occasionally superior, though it may not be acknowledged publicly. On the one hand, the wife can be called *sahadharmini,* "co-worker in doing duty"; on the other hand, husband and wife together can be called *dampatis,* "joint owners of the household." In one breath the ancient lawgiver Manu is quoted as giving women a subordinate position: "Her father protects her in childhood, her husband protects her in youth, her sons protect her in old age. A woman does not deserve independence." In another breath, Manu is said to have placed women on a high pedestal: "Where women verily are honored there the gods rejoice; where however they are not honored there all sacred rights prove fruitless."[19] In still other characterizations of women, Hindu tradition sees women as subtly dominant, even though their husbands seem outwardly to make the critical decisions of life. One popular story is recounted by Professors Paul and Susanna Ooommen Younger. Two *rajas* (kings) in southern India were playing a long game of chess, vying for the championship. The wife of the host was sitting nearby, rocking her baby and singing a lullaby. Noticing that her husband was about to make a wrong move, she signaled him a critical clue by subtly changing the words of her song. He got the message, changed his course, and won the title. "This story gives some insight into the nature of the husband-wife relationship," write the Youngers. "The Indian words for creator, teacher, sword, mountain, and protector are masculine. The words for strength, power, salvation, and intelligence are feminine."[20]

In setting up the Tribhuvandas Foundation, AMUL Dairy had itself responded to the signals coming from women. Processes of discontent were translated into processes of strengthening dairy operations in the longer term. If Dr. Nair was right, the new education for women, though directed at *household* improvement, might also be a step toward more active roles for women in the "man's world" of dairy decision making. In this view, women were seen as facilitating change, even while social relations seemed outwardly unchanged. (Not all observers were so sanguine.)[21] Other signs of advances for women were evident within the professional managerial ranks at AMUL headquarters. Women were employed on the veterinarian staff, and one of the two top positions under the Chairman was filled by a woman, Amrita Patel, the Managing Director of Operations, herself one of the leading candidates to succeed Kurien.

And yet if women seemed to be achieving more prominence in dairying, and if future generations might be expected to go further, it remained a puzzle exactly why—in more than three decades of the White Revolution—so few of the local dairy cooperatives involved women. Out of the some 18,000 local dairy cooperatives in western India, only a handful were run by women, or even had *any* women on the governing committees. Women's education had reached a level of priority, but not their involvement. Even those who knew Gujarat village life best were not altogether sure why.

Perhaps an even greater source of curiosity were those few cooperatives in which women *did* step forward to lead.[22] Over the years Khadgodhara village had been one of the more striking. There women had taken leadership initiative from an early stage. V. H. Shah arranged for a meeting with the woman who had founded the cooperative at Khadgodhara, one Jasumatiben Mehta. In 1967 Mrs. Mehta went against the flow of established male-female sensibilities and did what men in her village had tried to do and failed. After organizing about 100 milk producers, all women, she persuaded AMUL officials to formally recognize her group as an operating milk cooperative society. Village men opposed the move, but by sheer force of character, it was said, Mrs. Mehta prevailed. For years Khadgodhara's women had been walking the usual two kilometers morning and night to deliver milk to collection points; now they would have their own village-based station, with machines installed to test the fat content and enable dairy officials to pay women on the spot, ending years of wasted hours on the road. With the new system, coop members could deliver more milk, increasing the village's total daily milk receipts from about 2,000 to about 4,000 rupees and virtually doubling yearly household income. Mrs. Mehta encouraged women of all castes to join, including Muslims and untouchables. After eight years as chairperson of the society, Mrs. Mehta turned over the reins to a Muslim, then several Hindus, then a Muslim again.

Khadgodhara lay 60 kilometers northwest of Anand. All along the highway, signs called attention to the faces of candidates running for local office. Thirty years after being instituted by law, Gandhi's one-person, one-vote principle still remained in force. "Mrs. Mehta is herself a Gandhian from way back," explained V. H. Shah. "Following Gandhi's own practice, she reads through the sacred legend of Hindu scriptures, the Bhagavad Gita, two times each month.[23] It clearly propels the public service work she does, including the milk society." The road into the northern flatlands of Gujarat occasionally passed crossroads decorated with India's kaleidoscopic mix of odd visual bedfellows—shrines to Vishnu and Hari Krishna, billboards for cigarettes, a Christian church, traders hawking old fruit, people bathing naked at outdoor springs. V. H. Shah stopped the car at a railroad crossing, as a dilapidated train overflowing with passengers sped by. "Mrs. Mehta is high caste, a Brahmin," he explained, "so from birth she had advantages in status. But she was widowed at only 28 and left to raise three daughters. Though she had some land and was entitled by her caste to receive financial help and services from lower-caste villagers, she has always taken the initiative to do things for people of the other castes. Again, clearly a carryover from Gandhi."

Approaching Khadgodhara, the fields got visibly drier, the greenery of young wheat in the well-watered areas now giving way to the earth tones of cotton and cactus. In the drylands, income from dairying was particularly critical; if rains and crops were to fail, as they sometimes did, households would have to subsist on milk alone. Overhead, power lines followed even the remoter roadways, right into Khadgodhara itself. "One other thing you should know about Mrs. Mehta," said V. H. Shah, "is that she has not only run the milk cooperative society over the years, but also gained enough respect to become head of the village panchayat [council], and even got appointed to the panchayat of the district. For a woman to get that kind of recognition is unheard of. Yet for all her success in getting on councils, men have recently opposed her reelection to the council. And this is starting to put real strains on the efforts of women to run the milk society here."

Jasumatiben Mehta, now in her mid-70s, lived at the village outskirts in a modest dwelling next to shelters occupied by the families of two of her daughters. V. H. Shah parked the car in a small clearing next to several long-eared, hump-backed "Brahma bulls" and led the way to the house. In the late afternoon, the sun bathed the dirt streets in a golden light. Like most village structures, the Mehta residence was constructed of tree posts, mud walls, and corrugated tin roofing held up by columns of thin gnarled tree trunks. A white-haired woman and her daughters emerged from within. In all their simplicity, they hardly looked the "defiant exception to an age-old rule." Mrs. Mehta was a handsome white-haired woman with a gentle, dignified presence but unmistakable authority. Pulling her white sari up over her head, she signaled one daughter to bring tea out to the veranda. "When we first formed the women's milk society," she said, "you have to realize there was no milk society at all. Our women milked the cows and walked two kilometers every morning and night to reach the collection buildings. Once we had the cooperative, all kinds of things changed, much more than relieving women of walking miles. Women from all castes started to get involved. In the beginning, not a single Harijan household delivered milk to AMUL dairy, although forty of our 300 households were Harijan. But once we started the cooperative society here, they all started to come. Now we have members of all the castes—Patels, Rajputs, Harijans, Muslims, Christians.[24] Some Harijans have even served on the milk society council. Come, the milk society meeting is starting soon. I want you to see this mix of people we have on the committee."

Mrs. Mehta led the way across the village toward the milk depot, as multitudes of curious children skipped and danced at the wings. "By trying to serve poor people in the village," she said, "I learned to widen my outlook. I started to have lots of contacts with outsiders— all this came from involvement in the milk society. It's true for all the women members. For the first time they started to go out of the village, see the Dairy, see other institutions, inviting outside people to come here, getting more educated." She paused as some young girls darted by. "But I am disturbed, sometimes, when I talk with younger women and girls. I urge them to get involved. Many still say

John Schmerl

they are too busy with their work, on the farm, in school. Fortunately a few *do* get involved—they're my real hope."

To one side of the village, Mrs. Mehta pointed down the road.
"Harijan Street," she said. "Three milk society members are currently from this street, one on the management committee." She
turned away from Harijan Street and headed for the milk collection
station where the management committee was scheduled to meet.
"When it comes to the committee," she said, "our relation with men
has not been easy. In the early days they were even quite hostile.
Then, after only one year, we were selling enough milk to earn what
the gents were making from all their farm work combined. As we
started to make money, they became competitive and wanted to get
charge over the committee. We resisted. Several years later I stepped
down as chairperson, partly to get other women more involved."

At the coop building, the management committee was already in controversy. As dusk had set in, the debate went on by the light of oil lamps. The eight members of the committee sat in a semicircle, the new Muslim chairperson at the center. A young woman in her twenties, she wore a green full-length dress with gold trim that stood out from the saris of the Hindu women. Conspicuously present was her husband, who had opposed Mrs. Mehta in recent elections for village council. She won by a whisker, but the husband's appearance at this meeting was, for the women, a matter of no small annoyance. V. H. Shah whispered, "They're debating over contributions the society makes from its profits to village improvements. They think the committee should decide how the money will be spent—for the school, a road, the water tank. But some are saying the village elders should decide for them." Mrs. Mehta, though no longer on the governing committee, pushed forward her proposal that 1,000 rupees be contributed, for whatever project the dairy committee chose. Across the room, the chairperson's husband chimed in. "I don't think the milk society should have the right to contribute to village works," he said, "and in any case, the society should not contribute more than 500 rupees." His wife began to protest, when the secretary of the milk society, a senior male, jumped in. "No, the society *does* have the right to contribute to village works, but its decisions should be approved by vote of the village council." Mrs. Mehta, disturbed by the course of events, turned to V. H. Shah. "This will not be solved now. But you see the difficulties that come up with men getting involved. When you start to be profitable, it's hard for them to let money be distributed by the women. My only hope is that some day the younger women will be strong enough and stand their ground."[25]

■

The day after he received the 1989 World Food Prize, Verghese Kurien was in a reflective mood. "No, I am not satisfied today with the position of women," he said, leaning back in a chair at a conference room in an office block in Washington, DC. "In fact, correctly speaking, the dairy management committees should be *entirely* women. The milk societies are the fruit of their labor. And I think the local committees would be stronger—women are really better managers in this area." Kurien looked a bit fatigued, perhaps ready for the long-awaited retirement, though his breakneck schedule had not slowed a bit since the day when I first intercepted him dashing out of his meeting with the World Bank's president, a fresh $150 million loan in hand. "But I don't think you can push changes onto men in these communities. A massive learning process has been taking place—what a film about us once called 'churning.' It's a stirring up, and it takes time. Fortunately the churning at AMUL did bring to the surface one more thing we at headquarters could do for women—the education in nutrition and health. You have to watch for these opportunities over time—and *move* on them. But you can't expect too much change too fast for village women in our society. Operation Flood cannot be all things to all people. We can only hope for a more gradual progress, and more modest steps."

But in the long view of AMUL history, Kurien, in his reflective realism, was perhaps far too modest. The role of women had unquestionably changed, and drastically. Back in the 1950s the principle of separating people into different lines at milk collection depots not only applied to caste, but sex. Women could not stand in the same line as men. Operation Flood had changed all that. Gandhi's principle of one-person, one-vote had been translated by AMUL into the rule of first-come, first-served, with all persons standing in one line, men and women alike. The rise in women's income, in many cases to the level of their husbands', unquestionably increased women's role and responsibility in money matters. For widows trying to feed a family, the change was a breakthrough of major proportions. With one or two buffalos a widowed woman could earn a decent living, something never before possible. And the rise of a woman into the highest ranks of the male-dominated dairy hierarchy could not help but have ripple effects in the way women viewed themselves and their future.

As the future horizon now looked to Kurien, the churning over women was but one dimension of much larger transformations that lay in store. In the mid-'80s the dairy model—the "Anand Pattern"—was being extended to other industries, including the production and distribution of vegetable oils. It was a replication that Kurien fully expected to apply to other areas of production. The National Dairy Development Board's skills in refrigeration, transportation, and marketing of fresh produce were already helping to give rural vegetable producers in northern India access to the vast urban markets of New Delhi. And if Kurien had his way, the decentralized organization of dairying cooperatives would spill over further and influence the fundamental power relations of the country. "We should decentralize the provision of all kinds of services so that the people who provide the services are responsible to those who get them," he said. "We're already seeing this, as the people who provide electricity consider using the model of dairy cooperatives, with institutions owned by the people, reporting to the people they serve. It's just not possible for these huge government bureaucracies in Delhi to be sensitive to local needs. Better to make persons responsible to farmers in the village. Put a meter at every village, allow villagers to distribute the energy, and things will be done more efficiently. Energy, milk, food systems—I see a plurality of institutions emerging, not single centralized ones."

What international influence the Anand Pattern might have was far from clear. But by the start of the last decade of the twentieth century, it appeared that the Pattern would spill far beyond India's borders. Representatives of six Asian countries—China, Pakistan, the Philippines, Indonesia, Vietnam, and India—had begun talks in Gujarat to set up an international training center to replicate the Anand Pattern across Asia. Perhaps nothing could have pleased Kurien more than seeing the Anand Pattern replicated outside India. But outwardly he remained cautious about the image of the "new flood" abroad, as if conscious that the Gujarati farmers who gave him his job were still watching over his shoulder, and village women were, in their own way, looking on too. "It's not fitting," he said, "for a country like ours to become a provider of food aid or an exporter of dairy products when we've still got so much hunger and poverty at home. But I do think we can try to help our neighbors to see that the region does better, do a neighborly act. Training people in the Anand Pattern is our way of contributing. Even the poorest of our members can take pride in that. Someday, when the benefits spread all across Asia, some poor woman in Gujarat will say, my—I, too—dairy played a part in that."[26]

1. "One Man's Miracle: From a Trickle to a Flood," a film produced by Kalish Communications, Washington, DC, 1989.

2. Claude Alvares, "Operation Flood: The White Lie," *Illustrated Weekly of India*, October 30, 1983, p. 9. This article, quite critical of AMUL Dairy, was countered

by Dr. Kurien in an article by Dilip Thakore in India's *Business World* magazine, "Operation Flood: The Case for the Defence," Vol. 3, Issue 23, February 13–26, 1984.

3. For a good overview of the political origins, see A. H. Somjee, "The Techno-Managerial and Politico-Managerial Classes in a Milk Cooperative of India," *Journal of Asian and African Studies*, Vol. XVII, 1–2 (1982), pp. 122–134.

4. An illustrative discussion, along with a call for policy change, came in a presentation by Martha Fetherolf Loutfi at the 1980 conference on women in Copenhagen, later published by the International Labor Office in Geneva. Ms. Loutfi pointed out the inadequacy of programs aiming solely to increase household income, arguing the importance—if women were to be reached and standards of living improved in the household—of understanding who controls income within the household (*Rural Women: Unequal Partners in Development*, (Geneva: International Labor Office, 1981). For another pioneering article on the issues of income control, see Jane I. Guyer, "Household Budgets and Women's Incomes," African Studies Center, Working Paper #28, Boston University, 1980. The more general origins of concern over improving the status of women go back to the early 1970s, when the United Nations Commission on the Status of Women set out to increase public awareness of women's issues and in 1971 declared 1975 as International Women's Year. Momentum increased in the years that followed with passage of the Equal Rights Amendment by the U.S. Congress in 1972, legislation aiming U.S. foreign assistance more toward advancement of women, staging of the Mexico City World Conference in 1975, and the subsequent United Nations Decade for Women, culminating in the U.N. Conference for Women in Nairobi in 1985. For a good historical overview, see "The Challenge of Nairobi: Learning from the Past to Build a Better Future" (Report of the National Consultative Committee: Planning for Nairobi, submitted to the U.S. Information Agency, March 1985).

5. Findings in this regard began to gain recognition in the late 1970s, especially with the 1980 release of the first results of the World Fertility Survey, based in London. See Richard M. Harley, "When Women Want Fewer Children," *The Christian Science Monitor*, September 11, 1980.

6. Madhu Sarin explained in an interview: "I don't think we have succeeded in [establishing] really solid or proper participation of women in the overall decision-making process. . . . At first we were just thrilled by the fact that production was increasing and, instead of the goats, they brought in good quality buffaloes with phenomenal milk production and [the project got] extra cash coming in. . . . But because of the irrigation, production increased, and so has women's workload—more harvesting, more processing, more transporting from the field to the house, more care required for the buffaloes than with the goats. . . . They work probably twice the number of hours as men work. They are very tied to maintaining the economic viability of the family, but they are also working in agriculture, in livestock farming. Something like 70 percent of all agricultural work is done by women. . . . But the [situation of women in the aftermath of the Sukhomajri experiment] is extremely worrying. The men interact with the outside world, so women have very little access to information, they're very shielded, and [in effect end up being kept] as bonded laborers under the cover of [social expectations about their responsibility to the] family. . . . A big question confronting us is how do we ensure that even in a larger more systematic expansion of the program in many villages, women have a definite role in the decision-making process. And a lot of facilitation is needed for that because [the women's own assumption is that] my role is to be in the family, not to talk with [those outside]. . . . I think if you can help them get out of their isolation they

will start articulating all kinds of things to be done. They will take initiatives" (Interview, November 1989, Cambridge, MA).

7. As two of the most seasoned and insightful students of Indian dairying observe, "[The Dairy's] success, and phenomenal success, brought with it the dilution of the original purpose which was to help the poor. In its place came emphasis on productivity and on plans to replicate the organization elsewhere in India. The importance of none of these could be minimized. And yet these could not, and ought not to have become the *primary* concerns of an organization which probably represented the best in free India's social concerns. . . . At the organizational level, Amul was also under pressure from planners, policy makers, social workers, electioneering politicians, etc., to devise new strategies to help the poor" (Geeta Somjee and A. H. Somjee [of Simon Fraser University, Vancouver, British Columbia], *Reaching Out to the Poor: The Unfinished Rural Revolution* [New York: Macmillan, 1989], pp. 36–37).

8. The significance of electing the members of village councils, first instituted in 1957, stands out in bold relief compared to the history of nondemocratic patterns down the centuries. Professor A. H. Somjee of Simon Fraser University points out that the pattern of rule by self-constituted councils of village elites survived all the major periods of outside domination, from the Turks to the Moghuls to the Persians to the British. People became members of a panchayat according to caste and social position, and the panchayat's decisions were generally accepted by all villagers. For a time the British emasculated the councils of their judicial powers. After independence the Indian constitution revived those powers and reconstituted them on the basis of village elections—one person, one vote. This meant that, for the first time, persons of lower caste with little land could wield more influence in village society, since people of lower rank had the vote and could be mobilized for political support (Personal interview, Harvard University, January 1985).

9. "Independent India," he wrote, "can only discharge her duty towards a groaning world by adopting a simple but ennobled life, by developing her thousands of cottages and living at peace with the world. High thinking is inconsistent with complicated material life based on high speed imposed on us by Mammon worship. All the graces of life are possible only when we learn the art of living nobly. . . . At the same time, I believe that some key industries are necessary. I do not believe in armchair or armed Socialism. . . . [W]ithout having to enumerate key industries, I would have State ownership, where a large number of people have to work together. The ownership of the products of their labour, whether skilled or unskilled, will vest in them through the State. But as I can conceive such a State only based on nonviolence, I would not dispossess moneyed men by force but would invite their cooperation in the process of conversion to State ownership" (M. K. Gandhi, *Economic and Industrial Life and Relations* [Ahmedabad: Navajivan Publishing House, 1957], Vol. 2, pp. 19–20). In another revealing comment, Gandhi wrote, "Railways are there, I do not avoid them. I hate motor cars but I make use of them willy nilly all the same. Again, I dislike fountain-pens, but just now I am making use of one though I carry a reed-pen about in my box. Every time I use the fountain-pen it hurts me, and I think of the neglected reed-pen in my box. Compromise comes in at every step, but one must realize that it is a compromise, and keep the final goal constantly in front of the mind's eye" (op.cit., p. 13).

10. Kenneth Rivett, *Economic Thought of Mahatma Gandhi* (Bombay: Allied Publishers Private Ltd., 1959) pp. 7–17. As Gandhi himself once put it, "real art comes where we project ourselves in certain things, and cottage industries give us that opportunity, and every good cottage industry worker takes an interest in the work he

does himself" (in J. C. Kumparappa, *Gandhian Economic Thought* [Bombay: Vora & Co., Publishers Ltd., 1951], p. 39).

11. M. K. Gandhi, *Women and Social Injustice* (Ahmedabad: Navajivan Publishing House, 1942), p. 28.

12. For the nationalist political leaders, see note 3 above. Kurien's own involvement in dairying began in the early 1950s. After completing graduate study in the United States in physics and metallurgy at Michigan State University, he returned to India to take a government job setting up a powdered milk plant in Anand. He was soon approached by local farmers whose milk cooperatives were foundering. Seeing their frustration over failing, outdated machinery, and unsupportive government officials, he began offering the farmers help in off hours, introducing pasteurizing equipment and teaching them how to use it. The immediate results experienced by farmers convinced Kurien to give up his government post and work as the "farmers' employee" (Personal interview, Anand, India, January 1985).

13. A. H. Somjee argues that Kurien and the "technocrats" ran dairy operations with relatively little constraint on the part of politicians, even influential leaders of the Indian national movement, although these leaders played a very important role in pulling for the dairy movement in its formative years by going to villages, mobilizing public support for the new organization, and defending the technocrats before other politicians. Eventually, says Somjee, the technocrats came to define the public good in ways that were traditionally the preserve of the politicians (op. cit., p. 130; see also pp. 128–129). Ramjit Gupta, Chairman of the Centre for Agricultural Management at the Indian Institute of Management, observes that—apart from the legacy of Gandhi's support for decentralized organization—cooperative organization may also be a practical *business* necessity for Indian dairying. "It seems to me that organizationally there is no alternative because cooperatives provide you with economies of scale and the ability to have modern technology and modern management. And there is clear evidence that whenever this had happened the income of the small farmer doubled, trebled, and the overall social environment has improved as well. We have evolved a system of resources and distribution in India which is appropriate in many of the developing countries. This is to say that you have a large number of very small farmers, or marginal farmers. And this pattern is not going to change dramatically over time—even in a time horizon of 50 or 60 years. And the industrial goal will not be able to absorb a large part of the agricultural population. You have to find ways and means by which to provide better incomes or better standards of life to these people. To do this you have to have an organization which can move forward your technology and management of it, and the best form for us is the cooperative form. There is no other form which will work, in which the farmer will tend to his own crops, in which he will begin to control and manage resources, and will have input into the decisions which will affect his own welfare" (Interview, January 1987).

14. In one sense, Kurien's language of decentralization did not quite fit the reality of AMUL Dairy. Kurien knew how to wield centralized bureaucratic control and had done it for decades. He had built a highly efficient organization run by a highly trained cadre of professional managers operating in bureaucratic lockstep. Yet over the years he tried not to lose his orientation toward farmers. In 1964 Prime Minister Lal Bahadur Shastri asked Kurien to go to New Delhi, take charge of the National Dairy Development Board and operations, and replicate the "Anand Pattern" all over India. Kurien took the job, but only when he got the Prime Minister to agree that national dairy headquarters be based in Anand, and that Kurien serve at no salary lest he get too beholden to government. It was a leadership role, and a set of conditions, that

would remain in force more than twenty-five years. "I declined pay," he said, "because then my orientation would change. Every night before I go to bed I have to think whether today the farmers have paid me so much, whether I have saved them any money in the decisions I took that day. I always worry because I have a very high standard of living compared to the farmers who pay my salary; there is a conflict. I like the good things of life and cannot work as a missionary. But that doesn't keep me from thinking constantly of this wide gap between those who pay my salary and my lifestyle. So I would not shift my hiring arrangement to the government; I must constantly have the pressure of the farmers' interests bearing in on me. Then, I told the Prime Minister, Anand needs to be the headquarters for the National Dairy Development Board because there we could think about one thing—dairying, while in Delhi there were too many political pressures bearing in. It would distract us from the work" (Interview in Anand, Gujarat, India; January 1985). The National Dairy Development Board was originally set up by the government under the name Indian Dairy Corporation, primarily as a lending institution. Then it was dissolved and made a statutory corporation by act of Parliament, with Kurien as its chairman. Critics charged it was a classic case of industrial monopoly, with Kurien cornering power for himself and his colleagues at Anand (Alvares, op. cit., p. 12).

15. Some analysts have not been so sanguine about the effects on reducing the problems associated with caste. In their book, *Reaching Out to the Poor* (op. cit.), Geeta and A. H. Somjee illustrate in various ways just how resistant the caste system has been to efforts within the dairy movement to improve the benefits and personal involvement of the lower castes. On the general problem of caste, they write, "Rural communities in India have lived far too long with the caste system and therefore regard it as a necessary part of their social and economic existence. For them there always will be those who are socially higher and lower and also economically better off and worse off. And if somebody was excluded from the basic human dignity and economic opportunity, there were traditional explanations of *karma* for it. . . . So very deeply institutionalized is the karmic rationale in rural India, in the minds and manners of both the well-provided and the deprived, that there is very little questioning of it on either side. Only the social reformers question them but then after some time they go away and life goes on as before. . . . Indian society has yet to produce a mass movement, corresponding to its earlier national movement against the alien rule, which can generate leadership of the dedicated men and women who would then spread out into rural India, on a massive scale, and mobilize and organize the poor to demand, effectively, what has been provided for them in various plans and social policies, and also help them develop their social and political capacity by means of involvement in development and participatory processes and bring about their own self-development through self-involvement. The students of society and politics of India are now beginning to understand the colossal damage done by the Indian caste system to the lower strata of its society. It simply devastated them, and even took away their will to fight back for human dignity and social justice" (op. cit., pp. 37–39).

16. First made operational in 1980, by the mid-'80s the programs of the Tribhuvandas Foundation had begun to flourish. The Foundation was spending nearly 5 million rupees for educational programs in maternal and infant care, supplementary feeding, young farmer training, day care, family planning, immunization, sanitation, environmentally sound cooking practices, and other services (*Tribhuvandas Foundation Annual Report*, Anand, 1985). In establishing the Foundation, AMUL was moving more in the direction of so-called integrated rural development, responding on a variety of fronts to needs that were seen to be interconnected. In so doing, the Dairy

was countering one of the powerful lessons of international experience: the failure of many development strategies that tried to meet too many needs at once and became financially unwieldy, or financially unsustainable, in the long run. Ironically, as the Tribhuvandas Foundation was being established in the early '80s, development theorists Bruce F. Johnston and William C. Clark were complimenting AMUL Dairy and the National Dairy Development Board as a premier development strategy that had succeeded by concentrating on one major area of service and avoiding the dangers besetting organizations that tried to do too many things at once (*Redesigning Rural Development: A Strategic Perspective* [Baltimore & London: The Johns Hopkins University Press, 1982], p. 169.) Nevertheless, AMUL and the National Dairy Development Board had reached such organizational and financial strength that they seemed able to bear contributions to, and support for, the Foundation. Apparently the directors saw in the health program a way of enhancing the commitment and support of coop members, so strengthening the central purpose of the Dairy in the long run.

17. Long before setting up the Tribhuvandas Foundation, Kurien and Foundation originator Tribhuvandas K. Patel were aware of the problem of child malnutrition in Gujarat. By the 1970s the annual rate of infant deaths (many related to causes of malnutrition) was running about 144 per thousand—one of the highest rates in all of India (*Child in India: A Statistical Portrait* [New Delhi: Ministry of Welfare, Government of India, 1985], p. 155). Kurien had taken considerable pride that his dairy scheme made safe milk widely available in the villages and cities, and was convinced that it had made a great contribution to nutrition. His critics argued that the scheme was encouraging women to sell milk that would otherwise be used in the household, thus contributing to a fall in mother and child health (noted below). But few doubted the benefits of putting hard cash in the hands of women, enabling them to buy household goods, including food—food that would not otherwise have been available. Nevertheless, until the late 1970s it was not clear why malnutrition and infant mortality persisted. The realization emerged that the malnutrition culprit was not so much a lack of funds or a lack of milk but a lack of *education*. Unhealthy practices persisted everywhere—women putting their babies to breast after cleaning the nipple with cloth dipped in unclean water, only to find the baby coming down with diarrhea; cutting the umbilical cord with unclean instruments; women failing to wean their babies to solid foods at the normal six months, but continuing to breast-feed until eighteen months; women holding too much milk in the household when they could sell it, earn money, and improve the family diet with protein-rich vegetables; women using household milk not for child feeding but for adults and their afternoon tea. The problems of child health could not but look bad against the rising financial success of the dairy scheme. By the late 1970s Kurien and his senior colleagues sensed the time had come to set up a foundation to address the educational needs. (On criticisms of the nutritional impact of the National Dairy Development Board, see Claude Alvares, op. cit., pp. 10–11; refuted by Dr. Kurien and his colleagues in an article by Dilip Thakore, "Operation Flood: The Case for the Defence," *Business World* magazine [Bombay: Published for Ananda Bazar Patrika, Ltd.], Vol. 3, Issue 23, Feb. 13–26, 1984, pp. 35–53.) An independent survey of the literature on AMUL Dairy in 1987 concluded that "the paucity of evidence about the effects of dairy development on nutrition allows both proponents and critics to make unsubstantiated claims. However, changes in the consumption of milk—an item that is not generally a major or cost-effective source of nutrients for the poor—should not be central to the evaluation of Operation Flood. Of much greater importance is the program's effect on production, incomes, and total nutrient consumption" (H. Alderman, G. Mergos, and R. Slade,

Cooperatives and the Commercialization of Milk Production in India: A Literature Review [Washington, DC: International Food Policy Research Institute, 1987], p. 74).

18. UNICEF estimated that some 38,000 children under the age of five die each day, perhaps as many as two-thirds of the deaths being related to malnutrition-linked causes that are readily curable ("UNICEF: Facts and Figures 1989" [New York: UNICEF, 1989], a brochure). On the remarkably low cost of existing methods to protect children's lives (such as oral rehydration therapy) and the benefits for mothers in the developing world, see UNICEF's *State of the World's Children* (New York: Oxford University Press, 1986).

19. Paul Younger and Susanna Ooommen Younger, *Hinduism* (Niles, IL: Argus Communications, 1978), p. 70.

20. Op. cit., p. 70.

21. Some astute observers of Indian village life caution against forcing urban ideas on rural women. Said Dr. Kamla Chowdhry, director of the Society for the Promotion of Wastelands Development, "I don't want to see women pushed into significant decision-making roles. To push for them to take those roles because we in the urban areas say so, would be wrong. When they *want* it, yes, but not until then. The key issues village women are interested in are different—they're concerned about issues of the availability of fuel wood, fodder, and water. We should do something here to let women get involved, but not so much decisions of village councils" (Interview, New Delhi, January 1987).

22. The Somjees describe the experience of Dudhsagar (among other villages), one of the more interesting areas where women became actively involved (*Reaching Out to the Poor*, op. cit., pp. 50–55). The book includes useful statistics on the actual financial improvement experiences of various groups within village society in various locations.

23. A major theme of the Bhagavad Gita involves living up to the natural, divine rules of right living (*dharma*), even at great personal sacrifice and irrespective of consequences, leaving the outcome to divine providence.

24. Generally speaking, the region's social castes include (from top to bottom) (1) Brahmins, descendants of the priests; (2) upper-crust Rajputs, or descendants of land-owners and feudal lords, now deprived of much of their economic and political influ-ence; (3) Patels, or the landowning caste, involved in a range of activities from agricul-ture to commerce to small-scale industry; (4) Shatriyas, a mixture of upper-crust Rajputs and lower-caste Kolis who have become the most numerous and increasingly more powerful villagers, owning small plots and imitating the Patels; (5) various service castes (barbers, carpenters); (6) lower castes (not quite untouchables); (7) Harijans, or untouchables.

25. The Somjees (op. cit., pp. 24–28) include a fascinating description of the inter-nal dynamics set in motion at Khadgodhara when women got involved in the dairy coop and other areas of village decision making. For one thing, men began to feel threatened as women encroached upon their traditional leadership domains in the village. "[T]he [women] veterans of the milk coop, who wanted to continue their activity in the public domain, started knocking at the doors of the panchayat [village council]. It was such a traffic, of the women veterans of the democratic process within the milk coop, that the men within the panchayat feared and resented the most. . . . Earlier [the men] had, albeit mistakenly, thought that they had solved the gender jurisdictional problem by agreeing to let women have a total say in the milk coop, in return for which they would tacitly agree to keep their noses out men's business in the panchayat" (p. 26). Also, note the Somjees, when leadership of the milk coop

passed into the hands of women who were not "socially or educationally impressive enough," consternation and caste-based discrimination set in on the part of the better-educated, upper-caste women. Like the men, the women of Khadgodhara "equated political capacity with higher ethnicity. Thus men and women of rural India engaged themselves in the game of social exclusion, with all the traditional, karmic and educational rationale to support their prejudices. They behaved as Indians have always behaved since the dawn of their civilization, that is by closing down the access to advancement and status for social groups socially below them" (op. cit., pp. 27–28).

26. Personal interview, Washington, DC, October 18, 1989.

Prospect

FUTURES UNPERCEIVED AND PERCEIVED

Journalists who observe development innovations around the world are frequently asked what difference these innovations could make, how the future looks when positive change is factored in. Some questions come from citizens wanting to know the implications for helping people abroad; others from experts who, immersed in the study of particular regions, want to know what the experience has been elsewhere. Both groups want to know if things are really as bad as they seem in media reports—saturated as they are with images of Third World disaster, revolution, and starving children with pleading eyes. The view from inside the programs we have called "exceptional performers" is, in fact, strikingly different from the common impression. To be sure, the hardship, squalor, hunger, and disease are still there. But so is *change* in the traditional order of things, a fundamental *reordering* of social structures that makes age-old "fixed" patterns of suffering appear not quite so fixed after all.

From this vantage point, the common image of the "hunger problem," and what is needed in the future, also begin to change, displaced by a new image that recognizes the demonstrated potential for raising productivity and living standards of the poor. It is an image that involves new, often surprising, understandings about the process of facilitating change, with direct implications for future actions by the aid-giving nations. A journalistic survey of emerging views must necessarily be fragmentary and impressionistic, only hinting at broader currents of change. But there is much in worldwide research to confirm the significance of these currents. Countering the forces of disaster and despair, the "new understandings" have

148

become a transforming presence on the economic landscape. They are upsetting common assumptions about the poor that have long perpetuated the poverty cycle, insisting that very different outcomes are possible when misperceptions change.

Unanticipated payoffs in collaborations with the rural poor

Many development researchers were cheered in the 1980s by news that some countries were investing more in agriculture, beginning to correct the overemphasis on urban industry that had left rural populations in decline.[1] But the new hopes for rural development also raised concerns about *how such investments would be made,* since historically, attempts to improve conditions in the countryside have been full of complications. Reaching out to the poorer, remoter farm communities generally required extra effort and expense. Even those development planners who thought the poor themselves might have some good ideas were inclined to exclude them from the planning process. It was tempting to think that knowledge could be developed at research stations and "transferred" to people in the countryside in a kind of "command" approach. Sometimes this worked.[2] More often, as we have seen, rigid formulas failed, especially in agriculturally less favored lands tilled by small marginal farmers. Although poor, these farmers and their families were coping rather admirably with difficult environmental conditions. They also had sophisticated strategies for countering economic uncertainty—strategies that could lead them to resist what the "experts" wanted to do.[3] When it came to helping these rural communities, development planners faced agonizing questions: Were they prepared to adapt their plans and research to the conditions these farm families actually face? Would they be flexible enough to interact with the poor and alter program priorities to accommodate local preferences, with all the messiness such interaction can bring into the process?

Leaders of the "exceptional" programs studied here *did* take the risk of involving the rural poor in planning. While such cooperation may sometimes be motivated by moral obligation, these reformers were convinced that consultation and collaboration were necessary for program success. What they did not anticipate was the degree of *scientific and economic innovation* it brought, strengthening their conviction even more. Old assumptions about the "backwardness" and "resistance to change" of the rural poor yielded to a new appreciation of their capabilities—their often acute understanding of local conditions, their willingness to adopt new methods and participate in research, even when the advantages were not altogether clear.

In Mexico, Plan Puebla agronomists ended up reorienting their research away from a single crop toward making small farms work better as a whole. In this they took a road less traveled, and some prominent researchers who originally supported the experiment withdrew.[4] But the agronomists came to realize that aligning research with farmers' concerns produced a crop of valuable scientific insights, not to mention methods *campesinos* themselves would actually use. Some research stations in Kenya had a similar experience with local farmers, and in Burkina Faso the result was a simple, but ingenious, tool for contouring land that vastly improved the prospects for success in more advanced agricultural research. In the Himalayan foothills of northwest India, collaboration between scientists and farmers created a model of land restoration that had eluded all the technological quick fixes imposed by government.

Unexpected innovation also came in efforts to improve economic incentives in the countryside, in our cases bank credit. The Grameen Bank of Bangladesh developed its group borrowing strategy through consultation with the landless poor. The results were felt not only in Bangladesh but also in rural Arkansas and urban Chicago, where similar schemes have been used. In Pakistan, local farmers generated ideas that proved critical to the "bankers on bikes" program, including the rule of issuing loans only in public village meetings, curbing the opportunities for corruption or favoritism on the part of bank workers. The program itself became an essential factor in raising national agricultural productivity and making Pakistan a major exporter of food. Many national policy makers may consider the costs and practicality of such people-oriented collaboration beyond their resources and personnel. But where it *is* possible, and done well, such investment can yield some rather handsome payoffs.[5]

The "Perplexing Unforeseen" as a plus
in the development equation

The finding that the rural poor can be good partners who opt "rationally" for "rational change" has given no small encouragement to development practitioners. But practitioners have been equally *discouraged* by the unpredictable, and sometimes confounding, difficulties that crop up in the implementation of rural programs, foiling even some of the better-laid plans. Part of the problem is that rural societies are not so predictably static as was once assumed. They are constantly shifting and evolving in ways that are little recognized by governments and outside donors.[6] Often the researchers, planners, and government officials who have visited rural areas to "become aware" have simply misread the dynamics of poverty—a phenomenon Robert Chambers once dubbed "rural poverty unperceived."[7]

Yet those involved in the high-performing programs seem to have endowed rural unpredictability with a new air of respectability. To them, unexpected problems have proved essential for the "learning process," leading to adjustments that enable programs, in the end, to work. In this, their experience has confirmed a broader trend in development management to replace rigid "blueprints" for change with "process" approaches, encouraging planners to move with the course of events, to be willing to redefine their measures of success, and even to change their basic goals.[8] The model developed at Sukhomajri village for stopping erosion and rejuvenating the Himalayan foothills could not have been devised without the readiness of planners to alter initial goals. What began as a simple "scientific" attempt to measure and control erosion by building check dams developed into a much broader exercise in achieving community-nature harmony. The initial goals, inadequate though they were, led to a clearer understanding of the destructive links between the village economy and the fragile hills. Adjusting those links made possible a win-win result. The same learning process also revealed that the early breakthrough in spreading the benefits of new water resources needed to change over time. The principle of equality in water distribution—at first crucial for convincing all villagers to participate in preserving the hills—eventually proved unwieldy to administer and unacceptable to powerful groups. Changes were considered and implemented. Initial disappointment gave way to revisions that were more sustainable in the long run.

India's AMUL Dairy and National Dairy Development Board encountered difficulties pertaining to women at a very late stage in the program—some twenty-five years after it began. No doubt these problems, involving household nutrition, had first begun to surface much earlier. Possibly the Dairy was slow to sense their gravity. But more likely, the village women were themselves unclear that the Dairy could or should help them deal with needs at home, and felt impelled to demand it only as dairying matured. Decades had to pass for the Dairy to achieve higher levels of animal care and milk handling throughout the multitude of villages. Only then would villagers be able to see clearly the gap between animal health and child health. It also took time for women to summon the courage to speak out, probably fostered by their tours of dairy headquarters. By the 1970s village women found it unacceptable to have their education in buffalo health outpace their education in family health. AMUL Dairy's willingness to adjust course and respond in the '80s—even at such a late stage in AMUL's history—not only benefited women, but may have neutralized a dissatisfaction that could undermine their basic participation.

In some ways, the new optimism about unanticipatable chaos was prophetically anticipated by economist Albert Hirschman back in the 1960s. He was observing Latin American projects that proved more difficult than planners expected. Often, he found, difficulties that, if foreseen, might have aborted programs at the start, ended up working to the *benefit* of the programs and their planners. In fact, the difficulties often sparked innovation and creative response. Just as eighteenth-century economist Adam Smith had spoken of a benevolent "Invisible Hand" that seems to promote progress in free market economies, Hirschman observed that a similar unperceived, benevolent principle seems to guide many development efforts, hiding problems that would otherwise discourage practitioners from venturing forth—he called it the "Hiding Hand."[9] Hirschman's principle of the Hiding Hand has been much confirmed by the experience of many high-performing strategies, certainly that of our exceptional performers.[10]

Examples of capitalizing on the "perplexing unforeseen" underscore the importance of *process* not just for empowering those who direct development programs, but for appreciating the ordeals faced by the poor themselves. The rise of unexpected difficulties often reflects the fact that communities are experiencing painful and wrenching adjustments in the course of change. The exceptional performers seem particularly exceptional in their *patience* during such adjustments, enabling them to discover more profound ways of resolving human need than might otherwise have appeared. Letting new goals emerge from experience, rather than trying to "plan" them all in advance, is a principle increasingly recognized in business management as well.[11]

Strengths for, and of, the politically weak

Appreciating the value of the "learning process" has perhaps been a necessary complement to partnership with the poor, for no true partnership can exist without allowing the partners to adjust—to learn how to change. Still other breakthroughs, themselves necessary complements, have come in the political arena. Severe political obstacles have traditionally impeded the poorer people of rural society from realizing the changes they want. Recognizing these disadvantages, Robert Chambers argued that development practitioners must acquire a new professionalism that "puts the last first." In fact, he said, "new professionals already exist" on the development landscape. "They are those whose choices of where to work and where to allocate resources and authority reflect reversals toward the periphery and the poor; whose analysis and action pass the boundaries of disciplines to find new opportunities for the poor; and who test policy and action by asking who gains and who loses, seeking to help those who are deprived to help themselves."[12] If such an ideal would seem, in practice, beyond the reach of any mere mortal, the leaders of programs we call "exceptional performers" gained international attention partly because they did much to embody it. By extending to the poor more opportunities for self-help, they sidestepped an overwhelming historical tendency of leaders to concentrate power in themselves and their organizations, which alienated the poor and slowed rural progress around the world.[13]

Those development practitioners who successfully create opportunities at the periphery tend to be regarded as in some sense "charismatic," their achievements being credited largely to their personalities. But in the case of our high-performing programs, to dwell on the leaders' personalities would detract from understanding a far more important motivation behind their work: a fundamental conviction that the poor have latent capacities which—when necessary preconditions exist—enable them to make their own demands heard in the larger society, and so advance a notch in the scheme of things. In this conviction, our "new professionals" positioned themselves as advocates for the poor in situations that, politically, militated *against* the poor. In some cases, this advocacy meant creating economic opportunities for the poorer segments of society, and getting those opportunities endorsed by government. In other cases it meant encouraging the poor themselves to organize and acquire the collective strength to speak to government. But in all cases, the new professionals seem to have been convinced that real development is a profoundly political process in which the disadvantaged—with some backing in high places—can and must do much more on their own behalf.

Some of our high-performing programs encouraged political empowerment of the poor by decentralizing authority and strengthening local organizations. They believed such decentralizing a necessary step if the poor were to find a voice and advance their goals against intimidating and exploitative local elites, or to achieve the "critical political mass" to get their demands recognized nationally.[14] In Bolivia and India, the leadership of CCAM and AMUL Dairy, respectively, promoted village-based cooperatives, encouraging local participation and responsibility for decisions affecting family security. The cooperative form of organization may be especially well suited to the processing of small-farm products in these areas (rice in Bolivia, milk in India). But beyond the suitability of form, leaders were convinced that locally based organization was needed for small farmers to secure their rights in the broader political setting—a conviction increasingly applauded by development sociologists.[15]

Though the leaders of CCAM and AMUL Dairy had similar motives in promoting local organization, they differed in how they exercised their leadership. In the case of the smaller, more localized CCAM of eastern Bolivia, Dudley Conneely first helped small rice farmers to form village-based cooperatives coordinated by a central coop with elected leaders, rotation in office, and watchdog committees to check corruption. Typical of many new-style professionals, Conneely personally *withdrew* from organizational work once the coop could stand on its own. In the much larger cooperative organization, AMUL Dairy, and the national system supervised by India's National Dairy Development Board, chairman Verghese Kurien *continued to play a central role* over many years, wielding enormous influence. Clearly, dairy operations of national scope require a highly professionalized central organization. But Kurien—for all the length of his tenure—deliberately kept his system based on a foundation of democratically run local milk associations. He persisted in subjecting candidates for top offices (including himself) to election by the cooperative organizations. And when assuming leadership of the national dairy board, he refused a salary from the national government, arguing that this was the only way he could keep his attention fixed on serving farmer interests.

From another perspective, poor-oriented advocacy can be enhanced by organizations that centralize much authority. The very existence of such organizations, when positioned in the right way, can give the rural poor a much more prominent place in the national agenda, and budget. Some observers stress that top-level advocacy from authority centers is *essential* if the poor are to have a chance to participate in their own development. Economist Paul Streeten draws a simple comparison to the American South: "The Supreme Court [had] to act *before* blacks in Mississippi could more fully participate."[16] In India, the centralized aspect of Kurien's dairy operation is itself illustrative. The national influence of the Dairy organization unquestionably gave village interests a much greater voice than would otherwise have been the case.

In Pakistan and Bangladesh, the new banking systems, by definition, *had* to be centralized and highly directed, or risk financial collapse. Yet the strength of their central organizations enhanced the cause of rural development with national and local power brokers not normally known to smile on small-farmer gains. In Pakistan, the system of "bankers on bikes" stood as a national symbol for the new priority of smallholder agriculture. Improved efficiency at the bank also made the international community more willing to sink loans into the scheme, enhancing the position of small farmers even more.[17] In Bangladesh, the Grameen Bank's existence as a visible symbol of needed improvements for the landless poor put an entire segment of the rural population on the national economic map as never before.[18]

However it finally is expressed organizationally, the new professionalism seems to measure success as much by the fulfillment of local aspirations as by the realization of national goals or the aggrandizement of leaders. The scientist-peasant collaborations in farm research in Mexico, Kenya, and Burkina Faso were largely attempts to bring local farmers and their aspirations into the agenda-setting process. Success would now be measured not so much by the degree to which scientific knowledge developed at the "center" was adopted at the "periphery" but by the degree to which research brought practical benefits to farmers under the particular conditions they faced. Again, it is a service orientation that has gained recognition in the wider research, and now has parallels in leadership training programs in the affluent nations themselves.[19]

Measuring success by benefits at the periphery can conflict with the tendency of leaders at the center to gradually acquire more and more personal control. Some analysts rightly question the sustainability of successes that hinge on "great persons." Either the rising reputations of leaders may go to their heads and hinder their service to the periphery, or the success of their organizations become so geared to the leaders' charisma that the success fades when the leaders are no longer present.[20] Leaders of the high-performing strategies studied here were not unaware of this danger. In interviews I was constantly struck by their wariness of becoming cloaked in some Gandhian mantle that would sap their commitment to advancement in the countryside. To the extent that their sentiments were genuine, they espoused an ideal that has increasingly been voiced at international conferences—the call for "catalytic" rather than charismatic leadership, and for greater "participation" by local people in their own development.[21] As Peru's Francisco Sagasti, Chief of Strategic Planning at the World Bank, put it: "We no longer need the charismatic leaders, the heroes, the ideologues. . . . What we need is a different kind of leadership, a leadership that starts from below, that pulls people in, that leads *with* the people, not leads [over] the people. . . . It requires a capacity for being a hero in a different way, a hero who is part of those whom he leads, rather than one who stands out completely."[22] Related sentiments against power-concentrated leadership might also be discerned in contemporary citizens' movements across Africa that are demanding multiparty government. Influential studies on foreign aid stress the need for more investment in "human capital" and building the internal capabilities of poor nations to direct their own development and rely less on outside support. All these developments merely hint at some far greater, if still quiet, transformations reorienting the measures of success toward those at the periphery of power, inadequately though these transformations are covered in our media today.[23]

An end to "ending hunger":
Orientations for the concerned citizen

Lessons from the exceptional performers suggest ways of thinking about poverty reduction in the years ahead. Not surprisingly, these can radically diverge from expectations fostered by media images of the developing world. The media tend to generate expectations that are either too low or too high. On the "low side," the cumulative weight of direful stories from abroad can lead viewers to despair that any lasting headway can be made, no matter how much we, with the best of humanitarian intentions, try to help. But such expectations would not match the reality of possibility among today's rural poor. The lessons of four decades of "development learning" have put people in the aid-giving countries in a far better position than ever before to facilitate reductions in world hunger, and in the poverty that breeds hunger. The question now is not so much *whether* to support further efforts, but *what kinds of efforts* make a difference, and so deserve our support. Here the lessons of experience from exceptional performers are just as instructive, if not more so, as the lessons of failure. They tell us that much is indeed possible through partnerships with the rural poor, through process-oriented strategies that incorporate feedback from the poor, and through creating a climate of political economy more favorable to people at the periphery.[24]

Some media presentations would, on the other hand, set expectations too high. Television campaigns to raise money tell viewers that if everyone pitches in, we can "put an end to hunger," sometimes even forecasting a specific time for reaching that goal. The worst aspects of poverty, it is claimed, can be ended "in a decade." Political rhetoric sometimes compounds the problem. One of the more striking instances came in a widely publicized speech by former U.S. Secretary of State Henry Kissinger at the World Food Conference in 1974, urging that—in a decade—no child go to bed hungry. On the anniversary of the conference, in 1984, the United Nations was forced to do a study of why global efforts had fallen so terribly short. It is true, historically, that rapid gains have occasionally been possible in reducing age-old scourges, as with some diseases. It is also true that food production, which has kept ahead of population increases worldwide, could feed all people quite adequately if gains were made in improving family incomes.[25] UNICEF has further shown that many of the 35,000 children who die each day from malnutrition-related causes could easily be saved, if the political will can be found. The possibilities at hand for rapid change should not be underestimated. But media expressions of optimism in appeals to end hunger too easily misdirect hope, and energies. Rock concerts to "end hunger" in countries like Ethiopia raise unrealistic expectations of quick solutions, paving the way for dashed hopes when results fail to materialize. The public is hardly to blame if aid fatigue sets in.

Much more important for realistic expectations about future progress are the lessons of experience with rural transformation, including those of the better-performing strategies. If experience teaches anything it is that advances in alleviating hunger involve a *longer-term process* of human development and transformation. This process cannot be packaged in neat units of time, but entails many unfoldings of *qualitative improvement* in human livelihood, over different periods of time, at many different levels. At top policy levels, reforms are needed to put into place the preconditions for rural development—national and international economic incentives, land reform, more positive urban-rural links, environment-related reforms, and other policies in combinations that will differ from country to country. But none of these top-level changes will *enact* the transformations the poor need to embrace at a very personal level;

their ascendancy over hunger involves a process of personal emergence toward better livelihoods. Such personal transformations will not culminate in a decade, or two, or three, but lifetimes.

People in aid-giving countries, then, must reframe the goal of ending hunger to better reflect the real challenges ahead. How do we support the developmental steps appropriate for *particular* communities, countries, and continents, given their particular states and stages of development? For many average citizens, supporting "appropriate steps" means supporting private development agencies that sensitively discern these steps and take a long-term view. For foreign aid agencies and governments, it means withstanding pressures to get quick results from aid programs and investing more in the training of local people who will facilitate longer-term social and economic growth.[26] In a time of budgetary cost cutting, some of the best investments the aid-giving nations can make lie in such training and education, building the "human capital" and in-country institutions committed to involving the countryside in national development.

In part, the value of such investment is rooted in the growing recognition within poor nations of the need for long-term capacity building. But it also stems from new international realities that have made such investment vital to economic *self-interest* in the affluent nations themselves. Increasingly, for better or worse, we in the industrialized world are "in it together" with the world's poor nations. The global economy has become so interconnected in trade and finance that no country can remain isolated from the prosperity, or lack of it, in others. With about a third of the exports of industrialized nations going to developing nations, jobs at home now depend greatly on the prosperity, or lack of it, in the world's agrarian societies.[27]

The prospect of "going it together" with poor agrarian nations over the longer term may seem much less palatable than an outlook of short-horizon, occasional, or quick fixes. But as Albert Hirschman might remind us, partnerships with the disadvantaged are capable of considerable positive surprise. By pointing toward a future that includes the poor, the Hiding Hand may force us to realize potentials for the global economy and culture we would not otherwise see. The breakthroughs abroad have already begun to unleash sources of innovation—in technology, environmental renewal, and poverty alleviation—capable of giving not just local communities, but the

global economy, a major lift. To the extent that such "lift" is now
essential for our own prosperity, not to mention its necessity for
easing suffering abroad, perhaps the time is near when the media
will view advances in rural development with a new openness, recognizing that even the remoter, quieter breakthroughs on hunger are
news worth reporting.

1. By the mid-1980s, signs indicated that developing country leaders were more
committed to achieving a better balance of rural and urban growth and that more
national resources were being invested in agriculture (Nicholas D. Kristof, "The
Third World: Back to the Farm," in *The New York Times*, August 28, 1985, Business
Section, pp. 1 and 8). The World Food Council also reported in 1990 that the international community has become more sensitive to promoting food security measures.
"The adverse international economic environment has impeded successful adjustment in many developing countries. . . . A growing awareness of the social costs
attendant on structural adjustment has resulted in greater attention to poverty- and
food-security considerations by the World Bank and the IMF" (in "Additional and
More Effective Measures by Governments to Alleviate Hunger and Poverty: Report
by the Executive Director" [Rome: The World Food Council, April 6, 1990], p. 2).

2. Especially where a new farm technology had a clear advantage over existing
ones. Farmers who could afford it would generally adopt what was being recommended in the countryside. For instance, Green Revolution technologies took hold
and spread rapidly in the more favorable farmlands of India. Even many small landholders, once they saw the success on demonstration plots, quickly applied the superior methods, although such acceptance was not true of all areas of India (Interview in
Washington, DC, October 1989, with David Hopper of the World Bank, who based his
comments on his experience in early efforts to launch the Green Revolution in India).
In Indonesia the use of seeds and fertilizers spread rapidly, partly due to enforcement
by troops.

3. National plans or strategies from outside planners can too easily be perceived
as alien, and quite actively resisted. As former Ford Foundation representative Goren
Hyden once observed about Africa, policies imposed by centralized government ministries often have had little force, since the state governance structure and programs are
not linked directly with the subsistence agriculture practiced by many rural communities. "In a situation where the state is not structurally linked to the prevailing
systems of agricultural production in rural Africa, and therefore any policy initiative
deemed necessary for national development is viewed by most producers as an imposi-
tion, the blueprint approach becomes really questionable" (G. Hyden, *No Shortcuts to
Progress: African Development Management in Perspective* [Berkeley, CA: University of California Press, 1983], pp. 65–66).

4. After Plan Puebla's goals began to shift from only increasing corn production
to broader goals of income enhancement and welfare, CIMMYT (Center for the Improvement of Maize and Wheat) determined that the experiment had moved outside
the Center's research goals, and withdrew. However, it did affirm that the experiment
should continue (William F. Whyte, "Participatory Approaches to Agricultural Research and Development: A State-of-the-Art Paper" [Ithaca, NY: Rural Development
Committee, Center for International Studies, Cornell University, 1981], p. 21).

5. More generally, national planning that has improved prospects for small farmers has also yielded some handsome national gains. Such was the case in Asia for the land reforms of Taiwan and the rural infrastructure and credit in Indonesia and South Korea, among others. In Africa, small farmer investments in Kenya, Malawi, and Ivory Coast were a significant part of national agricultural advances in the mid-1980s that were not experienced in the neighboring countries of Tanzania, Zambia, and Ghana (Kristof, op. cit., p. 8).

6. As Africanist Paul Richards noted in his study, *Indigenous Agricultural Revolution: Ecology and Food Production in West Africa* (London: Hutchinson, 1985). He pointed out that peasant farmers are always experimenting with new ways of doing things, creating a dynamic of change in the countryside that is not always perceived, let alone understood, by governments or donor agencies that try to "improve things" there.

7. Robert Chambers, *Rural Poverty Unperceived: Problems and Remedies* (Washington, DC: World Bank, 1980).

8. Charles Sweet and Peter Weisel raised this point in their article "Process versus Blueprint: Models for Designing Rural Development Projects," in George Honadle and Rudi Klauss, *International Development Administration* (New York: Praeger, 1979), pp. 127–145. Soon after, David Korten emphasized the importance of the learning process in "Community Organization and Rural Development: A Learning Process Approach," *Public Administration Review* 40(5):480–511. More recently Derick W. Brinkerhoff and Marcus D. Engle have argued that neither of the two poles process and structure is adequate; some combination of both is needed in development planning. See Brinkerhoff and Engle, "Integrating Blueprint and Process: A Structural Flexibility Approach to Development Management," *Public Administration and Development* IX (1989):487–503.

9. As Hirschman elaborated the point, "Since we necessarily underestimate our [ability to be creative], it is desirable that we underestimate to a roughly similar extent the difficulties of the tasks we face so as to be tricked by these two offsetting underestimates into undertaking tasks that we can, but otherwise would not dare, tackle. The principle is important enough to deserve a name; since we are apparently on the trail here of some sort of invisible or hidden hand that beneficially hides difficulties from us, I propose the Hiding Hand" (Albert O. Hirschman, *Development Projects Observed* [Washington, DC: Brookings Institution, 1967], p. 13).

10. Trying to take the "rural unforeseen" into account at the beginning of a development program is not easy, since by definition the unforeseen is not yet visible. It is only natural to gravitate first to field-tested methods that "everyone knows will work." Happily, even when the supposedly tried and true methods seem to fail, the Hiding Hand does not scrap them altogether; it channels their more useful elements into a more versatile framework for constructive change. In central Mexico the temptation was great to transplant Green Revolution methods that were so successful elsewhere. When these methods did not immediately succeed, they were not totally discarded. Instead, useful elements were retained, only in forms better adapted to social and environmental needs and far more sustainable over time. Similarly, researchers influenced by the Green Revolution tried to improve conditions in drought-racked West Africa by developing "high-tech" seeds that would give exceptional yields when exposed to fertilizer. Learning from farmers that they could not always get the fertilizer they wanted, researchers turned their efforts toward what was really needed: an "intermediate" seed that would perform *with or without* fertilizer. The Hiding Hand which first obscured problems and appeared to slow the wheels of

progress, now revealed its benevolent side. As goals were adjusted, what was valuable in the first attempt was retained, and the wheels turned even faster.

11. In his provocative essay "Substitutes for Strategy," Karl E. Weick of the University of Texas urged managers to avoid the trap of spending too much time planning and too little time acting, since the acting, he said, is what generates real outcomes (as opposed to speculations) so that new directions can be identified. Strategic plans, said Weick, are a lot like maps—they animate and orient people. But once people begin to *act* "they generate tangible outcomes in some context, and this helps them discover what is occurring, what needs to be explained, and what should be done next." The point is, it is not the *plan* that deserves the credit for bringing the needed meaning, but the *experience of the action* (in David J. Teece, ed., *The Competitive Challenge: Strategies for Industrial Innovation and Renewal* [Cambridge, MA: Ballinger, 1987], p. 222). In a similar vein, a seasoned observer of East African development commented that "[development is not] something that can be predicted and planned. Still, such have been the prevailing views of development in Africa over the last two decades. These orientations have created a bias in favor of new projects and towards a disproportionate dependence on design and planning as opposed to management and execution" (Hyden, op. cit., p. 207).

12. *Rural Development: Putting the Last First* (London: Longman, 1983), pp. 188–189.

13. As Harvard Africanist Pauline Peters put it, "A lot of problems in development have to do with centralization of authority, with governments getting strangled, as it were, with their own weight. This centralization of authority also strangles the emergence of creative sources of new leadership. What we're starting to recognize is the need to create room for more competition to arise, which encourages new ideas to follow" (Interview, May 1990, at the Harvard Institute for International Development).

14. Such efforts stand out in contrast to now well-known cases in which political problems were associated with local elites and centralized "command" approaches to "advancing" rural programs—the former illustrated by the famous Comilla experiment in Bangladesh and the latter by the Ujamaa program in Tanzania. With Comilla, local management committees set up to increase people's participation in their own development needed to be strengthened after local elites encroached on their powers. With Tanzania's Ujamaa, efforts to promote villager participation through local "familyness" (*ujamaa*) villages were overwhelmed by problems of overcentralization in the administration, top-down goal setting, coercion, and excessive bureaucratic control. See John D. Montgomery, *Bureaucrats and People: Grassroots Participation in Third World Development* (Baltimore and London: The Johns Hopkins University Press, 1988), pp. 89–92. The World Food Council notes that administrative decentralization is now under way in an increasing number of countries in Latin America and Asia. "In Guatemala, efforts to transfer central Government responsibilities and funds to municipalities started in the mid-1980s. Similarly, in Nepal, local-level "panchayats" are being given a key role in development planning, even overseeing the local-level activities of various line ministries. However, it is important that decentralization measures are carefully designed and implemented, to avoid transferring resources to self-serving local elites. Many countries have successfully increased people's participation by building up farmer organizations, which can act as a conduit for the supply of inputs and develop joint marketing, processing and purchasing facilities. . . . The increased production in Zimbabwe's 'communal areas' was in large part the result of strong farmer organizations" ("Additional and More Effective Measures by Governments to Alleviate Hunger and Poverty: Report by the Executive Director" [Rome: The World Food Council, April 6, 1990], p. 6).

15. For instance, the World Bank's Michael M. Cernea, in "Farmer Organizations and Institution Building for Sustainable Development," in *Regional Development Dialogue* (Summer 1987) 8(2):1–24. In another paper—"User Groups as Producers in Participatory Afforestation Strategies," World Bank Discussion Paper No. 70 (Washington, DC: World Bank, 1989)—Cernea pointed out that some kinds of local organizations are better than others for promoting sustainable development in certain fields of endeavor. More generally regarding decentralization in the administration of national development programs, see Dennis A. Rondinelli, *Decentralization and Development: Policy Implementation in Developing Countries* (Beverly Hills, CA: Sage, 1983), and John D. Montgomery, op. cit.

16. Streeten cautions against overestimating the power of poor people to "pull themselves up" without the kind of strong central government support given in countries like China, South Korea, and Taiwan. Streeten elaborates on the kinds of central government and other high-level actions needed to undergird greater participation by the rural poor in the benefits of development in "Unsettled Questions in Basic Needs," *World Development* (1984) 12(9): 973–78, and in *What Price Food?* (Ithaca, NY: Cornell University Press, 1981).

17. In terms of promoting greater initiative and choice by rural producers, ADBP Chairman Jamil Nishtar was also deliberately trying to empower farmers at the grassroots. The on-site availability of credit through "bankers on bikes," along with new information about innovative ideas from other locations, greatly increased farmers' options. Nishtar also took pains to include farmers in advisory councils at the highest levels in the bank. The extent to which their advice was taken, or ended up favoring some groups at the expense of others, is debatable. But involvement of these farmers at higher planning levels sent a signal to the grassroots that the views of smallholders counted in ways they had not before.

18. Even if the bank itself is not the only way to help the landless improve their lot, as some critics charge, the visibility it gives the landless puts pressure on national leaders themselves to deliver more for this forgotten, but very sizable, segment of society.

19. See *Putting People First: Sociological Variables in Rural Development*, Michael M. Cernea, ed. (New York/Oxford/London: Oxford University Press, 1985). An example of a "parallel" in the teaching of leadership and public administration in wealthier nations can be found in new programs at the Kennedy School of Government at Harvard University. Professor Ronald Heifetz and colleagues wrote that "Training leaders, using this approach, would consist of teaching candidates to gauge their influence as a function of their responsiveness to the trends in the followers' expectations. Specific techniques would involve learning about politics, public opinion polling, motivation, and team-building" (Ronald A. Heifetz et al., "Teaching and Assessing Leadership Courses at the John F. Kennedy School of Government," *Journal of Policy Analysis and Management* 8(3):539–40).

20. To the extent that the success of high-performing development strategies is due to the formidable personalities of their leaders, observers may rightly ask what will happen when these leaders are no longer involved. Will the capabilities and spirit of innovation they embodied be lost? And does that detract from the viability of their models for change? Sociologist Max Weber observed that, historically, the passing of a charismatic leader is often followed by a pattern of organizational forces and bureaucratization that "routinizes" what was exceptional about the leader's ideas, eventually dulling the innovation or even snuffing it out altogether. The leader's successors often do manage to "capture" the original charisma to some degree in organizational forms and practices, but their motive may be to legitimate their own power, thus

defeating the purpose of preserving what was innovative and upsetting about the hero's untraditional vision for change (Max Weber, in H. H. Gerth and E. Wright Mills, *From Max Weber* [New York: Oxford University Press, 1946], p. 262).

21. The "catalytic leadership" phrase will be familiar to participants at international development conferences in the 1980s, such as the International Community Development Leadership Conference in New York City in the summer of 1982. Among the vast number of articles on efforts to encourage the rural poor to "participate" in efforts meant to benefit them, see John D. Montgomery, op. cit.; Norman T. Uphoff, John M. Cohen, and Arthur A. Goldsmith, "Feasibility and Application of Rural Development Participation: A State-of-the-Art Paper" (Ithaca, NY: Rural Development Committee, Center for International Studies, Cornell University, 1979); Milton J. Esman and Norman T. Uphoff, *Local Organizations* (Ithaca, NY: Cornell University Press, 1984); and *Institutions of Rural Development for the Poor: Decentralization and Organizational Linkages*, David K. Leonard and D. R. Marshall, eds. (Berkeley: Institute for International Studies, University of California, 1982).

22. Interview, summer 1989, conducted by Michael Camerini, then with World Development Productions, Inc. Portions were used in the public television series "Local Heroes, Global Change," broadcast in the United States in May 1990.

23. For instance, the surfacing in 1990 of popular protests for multiparty rule in countries across Africa, including Niger, Ivory Coast, Gabon, Namibia, Cameroon, Kenya, and Zaire (Robert M. Press, "Africans Join Protests for Multiparty Rule," *The Christian Science Monitor*, April 11, 1990, p. 1). On the concern for "human capital" investment in foreign aid, see Uma Lele, "Agricultural Growth, Domestic Policy and External Assistance to Africa: Lessons of a Quarter Century," MADIA Discussion Paper No. 1 (Washington, DC: World Bank Publications, 1989). On the basis of the review by Lele and colleagues of loans from 1960 to 1985 by World Bank and other external sources to Kenya, Tanzania, and Malawi in East Africa, and to Nigeria, Cameroon, and Senegal in West Africa, they concluded that international donors (especially other than the colonial powers that once ruled these nations) "have tended to underemphasize the importance of investing in the creation and expansion of human and institutional capacity, while overestimating the utility of aid packages in the form of physical plant and expatriate technical assistance" (p. 41). Paul Streeten argues that the investment in "people development" needs to see people as ends, not just a means to increasing productivity (as some "human capital" investment assumes). See his *The Frontiers of Development Studies* (New York: Macmillan, 1972), chapter 4, and *Development Perspectives* (New York: Macmillan, 1981), chapter 1. The *Human Development Report 1990* (New York: Oxford University Press, 1990) of the United Nations Development Programme, the first in a series, departed from assessing Third World country progress by measures of GNP per person and also included criteria of education, access to resources and choices, and length of life.

24. The relative rapidity of progress in the poor nations is extremely important to keep in mind. As the World Bank's David Morawetz noted, living standards and education in the developing world (taken as a whole) advanced more in decades than they did in two centuries of development in the industrialized North. See *Twenty-five Years of Economic Development: 1950 to 1975* (Baltimore: Johns Hopkins University Press, 1977).

25. *Poverty and Hunger: Issues and Options for Food Security in Developing Nations* (Washington, DC: World Bank, 1986).

26. In his capacity as senior scientific advisor to the U.S. Agency for International Development, Nile C. Brady pointed out the dangers of short-term expectations in the

aid-giving countries (understandable though they may be), and of deliberate pressures from groups with political interests, that do not take into account the need for openness and flexibility in the development process. "When the long-term needs and goals of some development endeavors are modified to respond to shorter-term concerns of public opinion, the potential positive impacts of the programs on [development] may be severely damaged" (*Food, Hunger, and Agricultural Issues,* Deborah Clubb and Polly C. Ligon, eds. [Morrilton, AR: Winrock International Institute for Agricultural Development, 1989], p. 104).

27. As one analyst at the Harvard Business School put it, "Our prosperity now depends on whether the rural societies of the developing world can grow economically—and whether we as a nation can understand what it takes to support that growth" (Interview, October 1988, with Ray Goldberg at the Harvard Business School).

Index

About the Author

John Schverl

Richard M. Harley received his undergraduate degree from Swarthmore and his master's degree from Oxford University, where he studied as a Rhodes scholar. He has received awards for his writing on international development issues for the *Christian Science Monitor* and has acted as a consultant to various development agencies, including the United Nations Food and Agriculture Organization. He currently serves on the faculty of the Harvard Institute for International Development and directs the Boston-based television company World Development Productions, Inc.

128741